1995 YEARBOOK of ASTRONOMY

D1465266

1995 YEARBOOK of ASTRONOMY

edited by

Patrick Moore

MACMILLAN

First published 1994 by
MACMILLAN REFERENCE
a division of Pan Macmillan Publishers Limited
Cavaye Place, London SW10 9PG
and Basingstoke

Associated companies throughout the world

ISBN 0–333–61863–7 (paperback)

9 8 7 6 5 4 3 2 1

A CIP catalogue record for this book is available from
the British Library

Photoset by Rowland Phototypesetting Limited
Bury St Edmunds, Suffolk
Printed and bound in Great Britain by
Mackays of Chatham plc, Chatham, Kent

Contents

Part II: *Article Section*

Part III: *Miscellaneous*

Editor's Foreword

The pattern of the *Yearbook* follows the usual formula – something for everybody. Our authors include some who have been loyal contributors for many years, together with some whom we welcome for the first time – and, of course, Gordon Taylor has made his usual vital contribution of the monthly notes and data.

David Allen has written his usual splendid article. Most unfortunately he has been taken seriously ill. All of our readers will wish him a very speedy and complete recovery.

The main text of the *Yearbook* had to go to press before the July collision between Jupiter and Comet Shoemaker–Levy; we have been able to include a brief 'Stop Press', but hope to deal with this event more fully in the *1996 Yearbook*.

PATRICK MOORE
Selsey, May 1994

Preface

New readers will find that all the information in this *Yearbook* is given in diagrammatic or descriptive form; the positions of the planets may easily be found on the specially designed star charts, while the monthly notes describe the movements of the planets and give details of other astronomical phenomena visible in both the northern and southern hemispheres. Two sets of the star charts are provided. The **Northern Charts** (pp. 14 to 39) are designed for use in latitude 52 degrees north, but may be used without alteration throughout the British Isles, and (except in the case of eclipses and occultations) in other countries of similar north latitude. The **Southern Charts** (pp. 40 to 65) are drawn for latitude 35 degrees south, and are suitable for use in South Africa, Australia and New Zealand, and other stations in approximately the same south latitude. The reader who needs more detailed information will find *Norton's Star Atlas* (Longman) an invaluable guide, while more precise positions of the planets and their satellites, together with predictions of occultations, meteor showers, and periodic comets may be found in the *Handbook* of the British Astronomical Association. The British monthly periodical, with current news, articles, and monthly notes is *Astronomy Now*. Readers will also find details of forthcoming events given in the American *Sky and Telescope*. This monthly publication also produces a special occultation supplement giving predictions for the United States and Canada.

Important Note
The times given on the star charts and in the Monthly Notes are generally given as local times, using the 24-hour clock, the day beginning at midnight. All the dates, and the times of a few events (e.g. eclipses), are given in Greenwich Mean Time (GMT), which is related to local time by the formula

Local Mean Time = GMT − west longitude

In practice, small differences of longitudes are ignored, and the observer will use local clock time, which will be the appropriate

Standard (or Zone) Time. As the formula indicates, places in west longitude will have a Standard Time slow on GMT, while places in east longitude will have a Standard Time fast on GMT. As examples we have:

Standard Time in

New Zealand	GMT	+	12 hours
Victoria; N.S.W.	GMT	+	10 hours
Western Australia	GMT	+	8 hours
South Africa	GMT	+	2 hours
British Isles	GMT		
Eastern S.T.	GMT	−	5 hours
Central S.T.	GMT	−	6 hours, etc.

If Summer Time is in use, the clocks will have to have been advanced by one hour, and this hour must be subtracted from the clock time to give Standard Time.

In Great Britain and N. Ireland, Summer Time will be in force in 1995 from March 26^d01^h until October 22^d01^h GMT.

Notes on the Star Charts

The stars, together with the Sun, Moon and planets seem to be set on the surface of the celestial sphere, which appears to rotate about the Earth from east to west. Since it is impossible to represent a curved surface accurately on a plane, any kind of star map is bound to contain some form of distortion. But it is well known that the eye can endure some kinds of distortion better than others, and it is particularly true that the eye is most sensitive to deviations from the vertical and horizontal. For this reason the star charts given in this volume have been designed to give a true representation of vertical and horizontal lines, whatever may be the resulting distortion in the shape of a constellation figure. It will be found that the amount of distortion is, in general, quite small, and is only obvious in the case of large constellations such as Leo and Pegasus, when these appear at the top of the charts, and so are drawn out sideways.

The charts show all stars down to the fourth magnitude, together with a number of fainter stars which are necessary to define the shape of a constellation. There is no standard system for representing the outlines of the constellations, and triangles and other simple figures have been used to give outlines which are easy to follow with the naked eye. The names of the constellations are given, together with the proper names of the brighter stars. The apparent magnitudes of the stars are indicated roughly by using four different sizes of dots, the larger dots representing the brighter stars.

The two sets of star charts are similar in design. At each opening there is a group of four charts which give a complete coverage of the sky up to an altitude of 62½ degrees; there are twelve such groups to cover the entire year. In the **Northern Charts** (for 52 degrees north) the upper two charts show the southern sky, south being at the centre and east on the left. The coverage is from 10 degrees north of east (top left) to 10 degrees north of west (top right). The two lower charts show the northern sky from 10 degrees south of west (lower left) to 10 degrees south of east (lower right). There is thus an overlap east and west.

Conversely, in the **Southern Charts** (for 35 degrees south) the upper two charts show the northern sky, with north at the centre and east on the right. The two lower charts show the southern sky, with south at the centre and east on the left. The coverage and overlap is the same on both sets of charts.

Because the sidereal day is shorter than the solar day, the stars appear to rise and set about four minutes earlier each day, and this amounts to two hours in a month. Hence the twelve groups of charts in each set are sufficient to give the appearance of the sky throughout the day at intervals of two hours, or at the same time of night at monthly intervals throughout the year. The actual range of dates and times when the stars on the charts are visible is indicated at the top of each page. Each group is numbered in bold type, and the number to be used for any given month and time is summarized in the following table:

Local Time	18h	20h	22h	0h	2h	4h	6h
January	11	12	1	2	3	4	5
February	12	1	2	3	4	5	6
March	1	2	3	4	5	6	7
April	2	3	4	5	6	7	8
May	3	4	5	6	7	8	9
June	4	5	6	7	8	9	10
July	5	6	7	8	9	10	11
August	6	7	8	9	10	11	12
September	7	8	9	10	11	12	1
October	8	9	10	11	12	1	2
November	9	10	11	12	1	2	3
December	10	11	12	1	2	3	4

The charts are drawn to scale, the horizontal measurements, marked at every 10 degrees, giving the azimuths (or true bearings) measured from the north round through east (90 degrees), south (180 degrees), and west (270 degrees). The vertical measurements, similarly marked, give the altitudes of the stars up to 62½ degrees. Estimates of altitude and azimuth made from these charts will necessarily be mere approximations, since no observer will be exactly at the adopted latitude, or at the stated time, but they will serve for the identification of stars and planets.

The ecliptic is drawn as a broken line on which longitude is marked at every 10 degrees; the positions of the planets are then easily found by reference to the table on page 71. It will be noticed that on the Southern Charts the **ecliptic** may reach an altitude in excess of 62½ degrees on star charts 5 to 9. The continuations of the broken line will be found on the charts of overhead stars.

There is a curious illusion that stars at an altitude of 60 degrees or more are actually overhead, and the beginner may often feel that he is leaning over backwards in trying to see them. These overhead stars are given separately on the pages immediately following the main star charts. The entire year is covered at one opening, each of the four maps showing the overhead stars at times which correspond to those of three of the main star charts. The position of the zenith is indicated by a cross, and this cross marks the centre of a circle which is 35 degrees from the zenith; there is thus a small overlap with the main charts.

The broken line leading from the north (on the Northern Charts) or from the south (on the Southern Charts) is numbered to indicate the corresponding main chart. Thus on page 38 the N-S line numbered 6 is to be regarded as an extension of the centre (south) line of chart 6 on pages 24 and 25, and at the top of these pages are printed the dates and times which are appropriate. Similarly, on page 65, the S-N line numbered 10 connects with the north line of the upper charts on pages 58 and 59.

The overhead stars are plotted as maps on a conical projection, and the scale is rather smaller than that of the main charts.

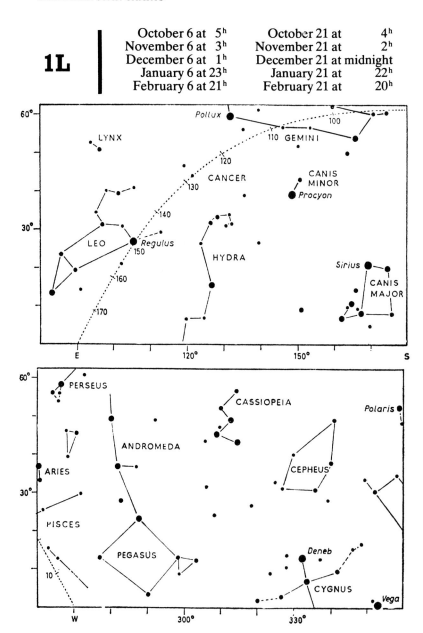

1L

October 6 at 5ʰ
November 6 at 3ʰ
December 6 at 1ʰ
January 6 at 23ʰ
February 6 at 21ʰ

October 21 at 4ʰ
November 21 at 2ʰ
December 21 at midnight
January 21 at 22ʰ
February 21 at 20ʰ

October 6 at 5ʰ	October 21 at 4ʰ
November 6 at 3ʰ	November 21 at 2ʰ
December 6 at 1ʰ	December 21 at midnight
January 6 at 23ʰ	January 21 at 22ʰ
February 6 at 21ʰ	February 21 at 20ʰ

1R

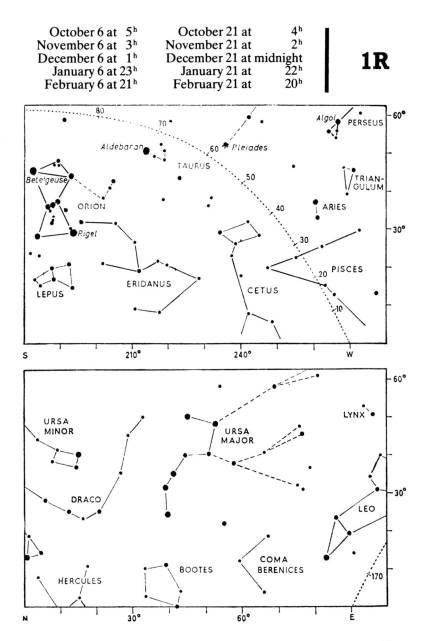

2L

November 6 at 5ʰ	November 21 at 4ʰ
December 6 at 3ʰ	December 21 at 2ʰ
January 6 at 1ʰ	January 21 at midnight
February 6 at 23ʰ	February 21 at 22ʰ
March 6 at 21ʰ	March 21 at 20ʰ

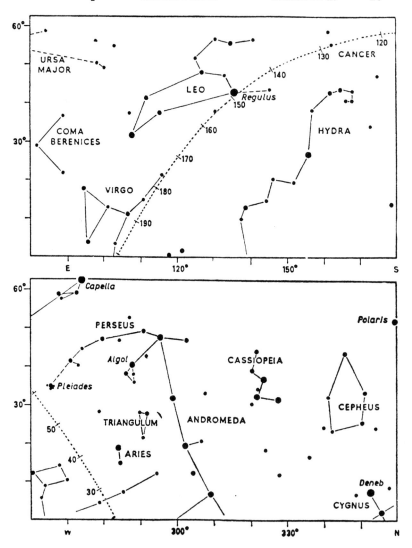

November 6 at 5ʰ	November 21 at 4ʰ	
December 6 at 3ʰ	December 21 at 2ʰ	**2R**
January 6 at 1ʰ	January 21 at midnight	
February 6 at 23ʰ	February 21 at 22ʰ	
March 6 at 21ʰ	March 21 at 20ʰ	

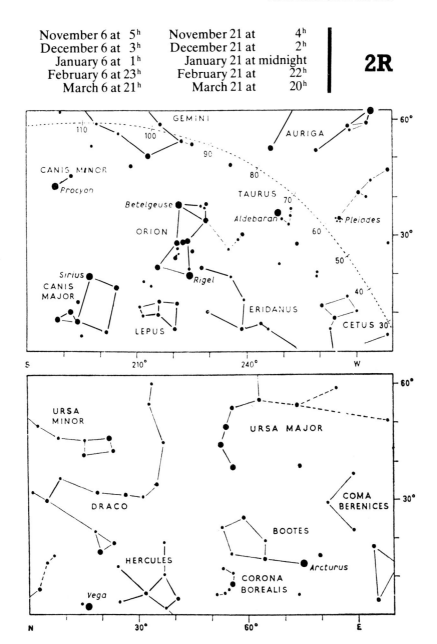

3L

December 6 at 5ʰ	December 21 at 4ʰ
January 6 at 3ʰ	January 21 at 2ʰ
February 6 at 1ʰ	February 21 at midnight
March 6 at 23ʰ	March 21 at 22ʰ
April 6 at 21ʰ	April 21 at 20ʰ

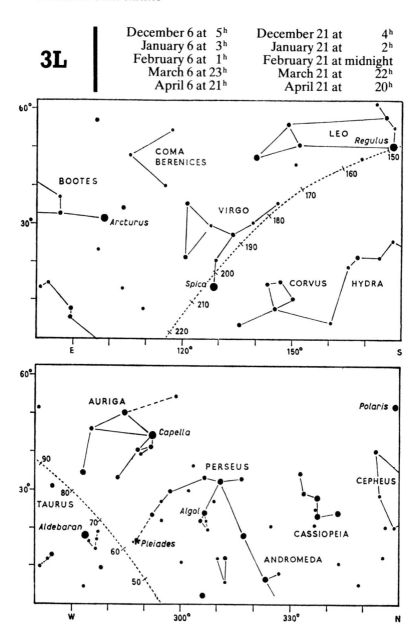

December 6 at 5ʰ	December 21 at	4ʰ
January 6 at 3ʰ	January 21 at	2ʰ
February 6 at 1ʰ	February 21 at midnight	
March 6 at 23ʰ	March 21 at	22ʰ
April 6 at 21ʰ	April 21 at	20ʰ

3R

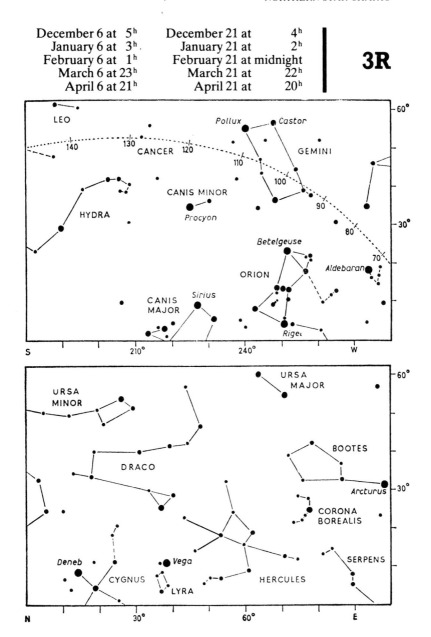

4L

January 6 at 5ʰ	January 21 at 4ʰ
February 6 at 3ʰ	February 21 at 2ʰ
March 6 at 1ʰ	March 21 at midnight
April 6 at 23ʰ	April 21 at 22ʰ
May 6 at 21ʰ	May 21 at 20ʰ

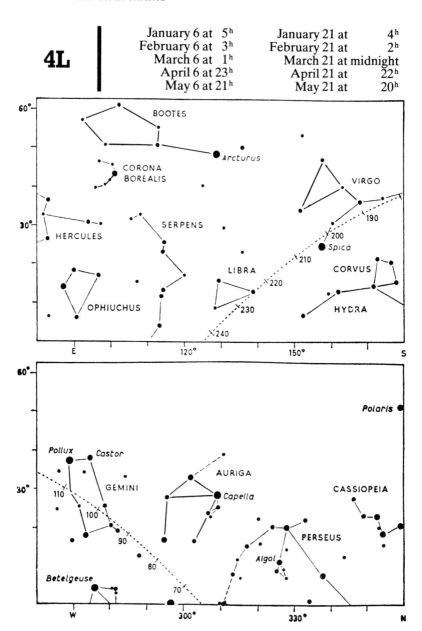

January 6 at 5^h	January 21 at 4^h	
February 6 at 3^h	February 21 at 2^h	
March 6 at 1^h	March 21 at midnight	**4R**
April 6 at 23^h	April 21 at 22^h	
May 6 at 21^h	May 21 at 20^h	

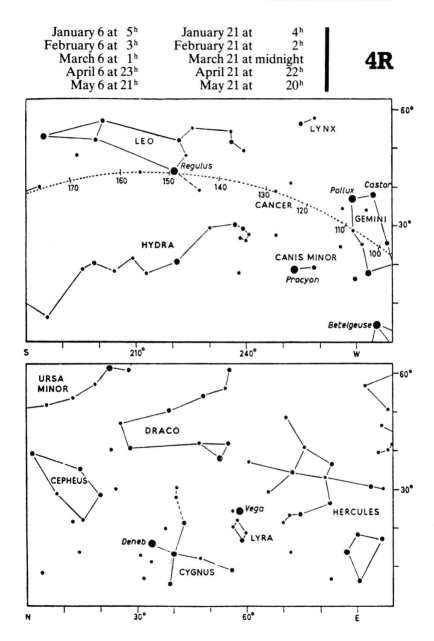

5L

January 6 at   7ʰ   January 21 at   6ʰ
February 6 at   5ʰ   February 21 at   4ʰ
March 6 at   3ʰ   March 21 at   2ʰ
April 6 at   1ʰ   April 21 at midnight
May 6 at 23ʰ   May 21 at   22ʰ

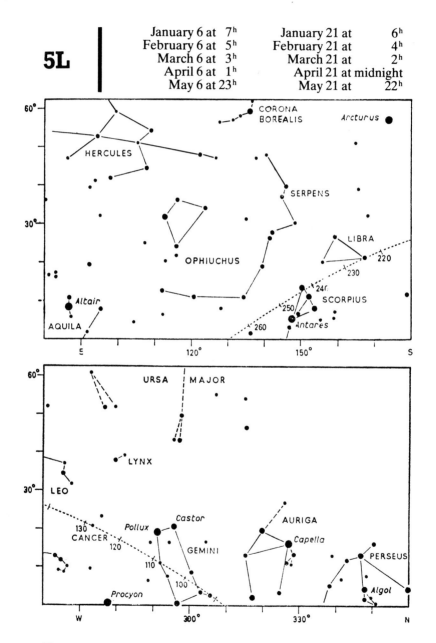

January 6 at 7ʰ	January 21 at 6ʰ	
February 6 at 5ʰ	February 21 at 4ʰ	
March 6 at 3ʰ	March 21 at 2ʰ	**5R**
April 6 at 1ʰ	April 21 at midnight	
May 6 at 23ʰ	May 21 at 22ʰ	

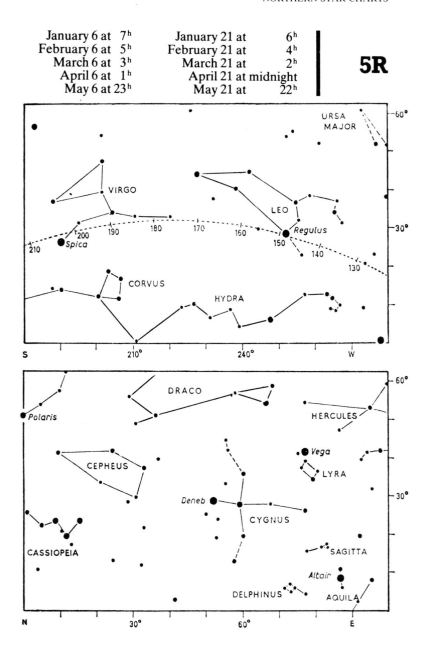

6L

March 6 at 5^h	March 21 at 4^h
April 6 at 3^h	April 21 at 2^h
May 6 at 1^h	May 21 at midnight
June 6 at 23^h	June 21 at 22^h
July 6 at 21^h	July 21 at 20^h

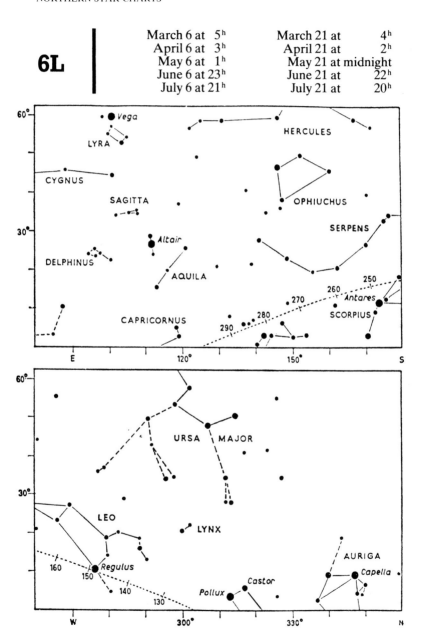

March 6 at 5ʰ	March 21 at 4ʰ	
April 6 at 3ʰ	April 21 at 2ʰ	**6R**
May 6 at 1ʰ	May 21 at midnight	
June 6 at 23ʰ	June 21 at 22ʰ	
July 6 at 21ʰ	July 21 at 20ʰ	

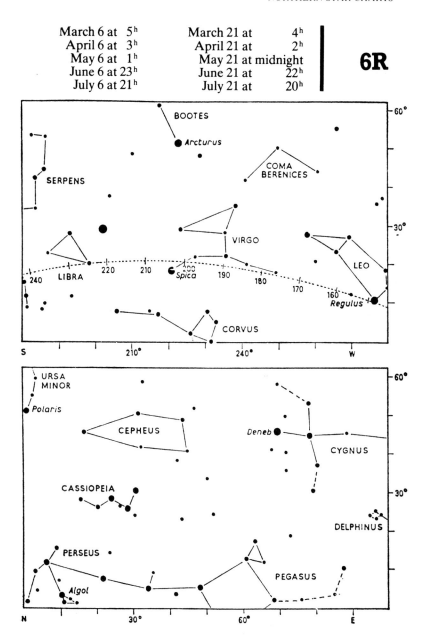

7L

May 6 at 3ʰ	May 21 at 2ʰ
June 6 at 1ʰ	June 21 at midnight
July 6 at 23ʰ	July 21 at 22ʰ
August 6 at 21ʰ	August 21 at 20ʰ
September 6 at 19ʰ	September 21 at 18ʰ

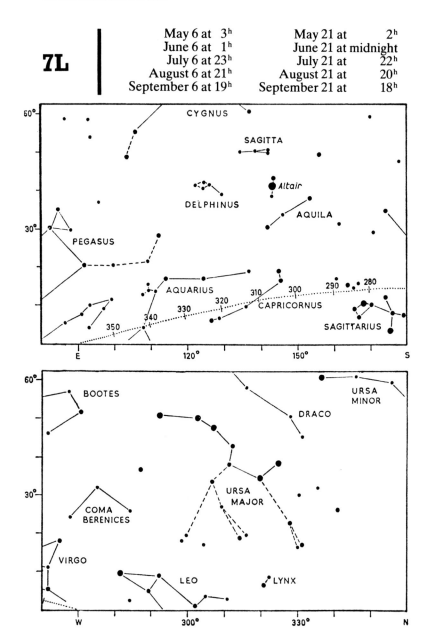

May 6 at 3^h	May 21 at 2^h	
June 6 at 1^h	June 21 at midnight	**7R**
July 6 at 23^h	July 21 at 22^h	
August 6 at 21^h	August 21 at 20^h	
September 6 at 19^h	September 21 at 18^h	

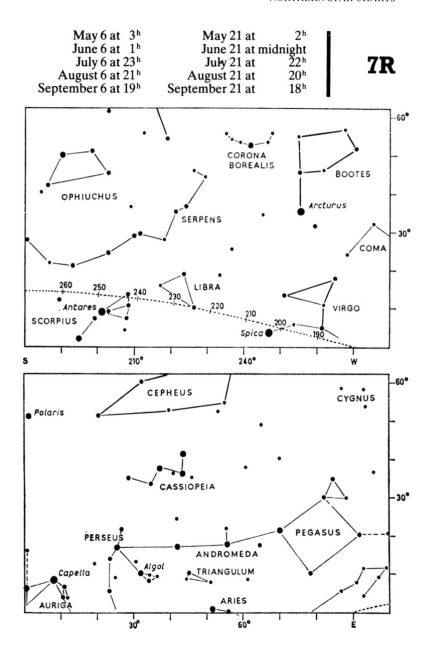

8L

July 6 at 1ʰ	July 21 at midnight
August 6 at 23ʰ	August 21 at 22ʰ
September 6 at 21ʰ	September 21 at 20ʰ
October 6 at 19ʰ	October 21 at 18ʰ
November 6 at 17ʰ	November 21 at 16ʰ

July 6 at 1ʰ	July 21 at midnight	
August 6 at 23ʰ	August 21 at 22ʰ	**8R**
September 6 at 21ʰ	September 21 at 20ʰ	
October 6 at 19ʰ	October 21 at 18ʰ	
November 6 at 17ʰ	November 21 at 16ʰ	

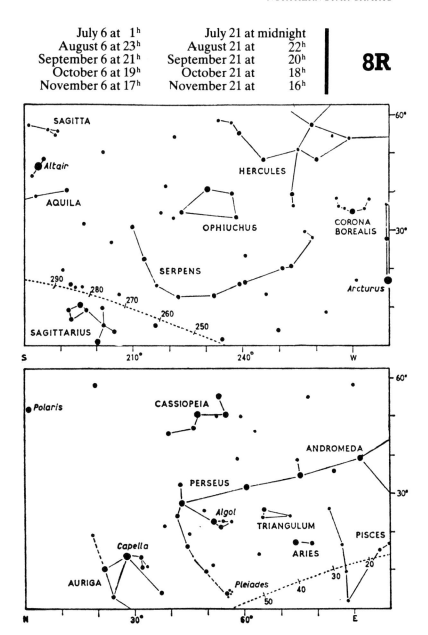

9L

August 6 at 1ʰ	August 21 at midnight
September 6 at 23ʰ	September 21 at 22ʰ
October 6 at 21ʰ	October 21 at 20ʰ
November 6 at 19ʰ	November 21 at 18ʰ
December 6 at 17ʰ	December 21 at 16ʰ

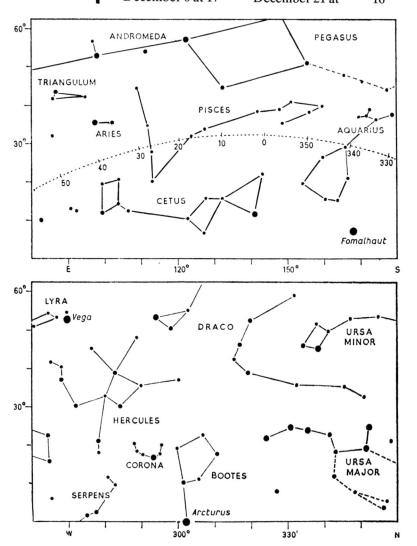

August 6 at 1ʰ	August 21 at midnight
September 6 at 23ʰ	September 21 at 22ʰ
October 6 at 21ʰ	October 21 at 20ʰ
November 6 at 19ʰ	November 21 at 18ʰ
December 6 at 17ʰ	December 21 at 16ʰ

9R

10L

August 6 at 3ʰ	August 21 at 2ʰ
September 6 at 1ʰ	September 21 at midnight
October 6 at 23ʰ	October 21 at 22ʰ
November 6 at 21ʰ	November 21 at 20ʰ
December 6 at 19ʰ	December 21 at 18ʰ

August 6 at 3^h	August 21 at 2^h
September 6 at 1^h	September 21 at midnight
October 6 at 23^h	October 21 at 22^h
November 6 at 21^h	November 21 at 20^h
December 6 at 19^h	December 21 at 18^h

10R

11L

September 6 at 3ʰ	September 21 at 2ʰ
October 6 at 1ʰ	October 21 at midnight
November 6 at 23ʰ	November 21 at 22ʰ
December 6 at 21ʰ	December 21 at 20ʰ
January 6 at 19ʰ	January 21 at 18ʰ

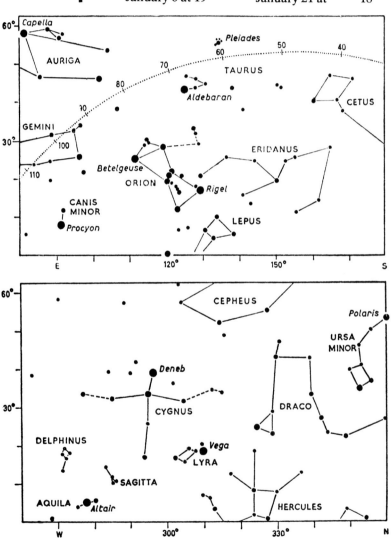

September 6 at	3ʰ	September 21 at	2ʰ
October 6 at	1ʰ	October 21 at midnight	
November 6 at	23ʰ	November 21 at	22ʰ
December 6 at	21ʰ	December 21 at	20ʰ
January 6 at	19ʰ	January 21 at	18ʰ

11R

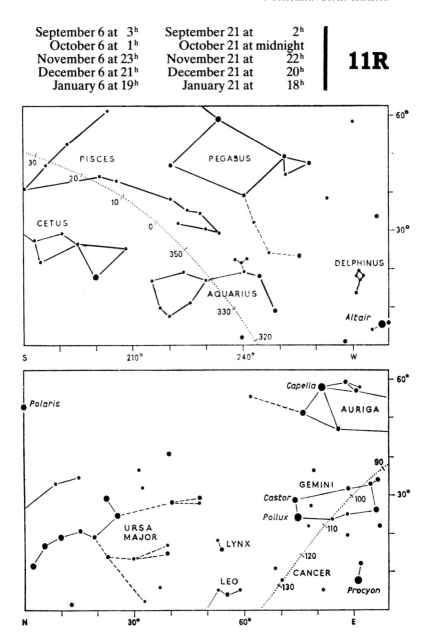

12L

October 6 at 3ʰ	October 21 at 2ʰ
November 6 at 1ʰ	November 21 at midnight
December 6 at 23ʰ	December 21 at 22ʰ
January 6 at 21ʰ	January 21 at 20ʰ
February 6 at 19ʰ	February 21 at 18ʰ

October 6 at 3ʰ	October 21 at 2ʰ	
November 6 at 1ʰ	November 21 at midnight	**12R**
December 6 at 23ʰ	December 21 at 22ʰ	
January 6 at 21ʰ	January 21 at 20ʰ	
February 6 at 19ʰ	February 21 at 18ʰ	

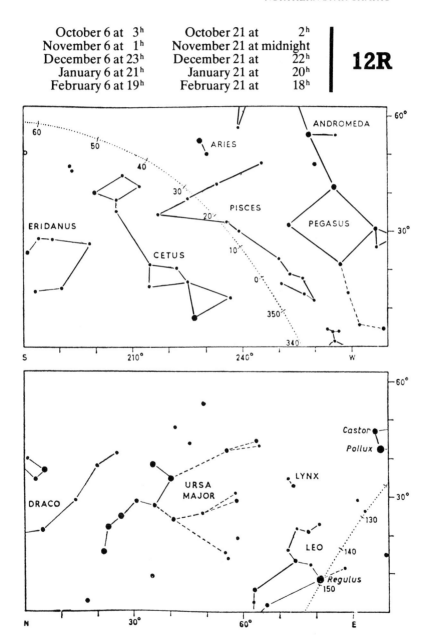

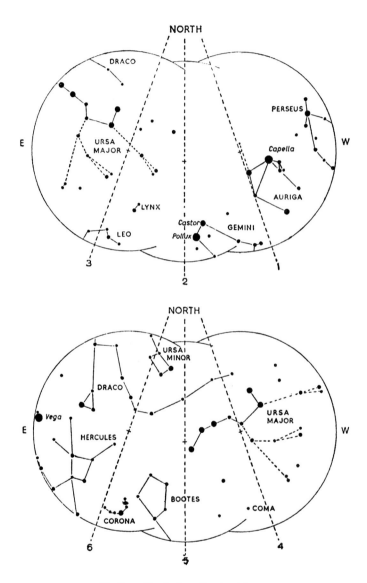

Northern Hemisphere Overhead Stars

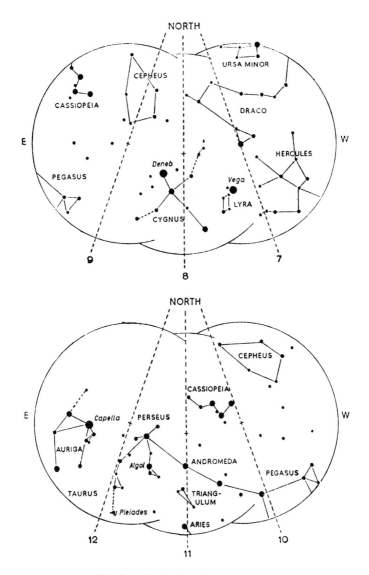

Northern Hemisphere Overhead Stars

1L

October 6 at 5^h	October 21 at 4^h
November 6 at 3^h	November 21 at 2^h
December 6 at 1^h	December 21 at midnight
January 6 at 23^h	January 21 at 22^h
February 6 at 21^h	February 21 at 20^h

October 6 at 5ʰ	October 21 at 4ʰ	
November 6 at 3ʰ	November 21 at 2ʰ	
December 6 at 1ʰ	December 21 at midnight	**1R**
January 6 at 23ʰ	January 21 at 22ʰ	
February 6 at 21ʰ	February 21 at 20ʰ	

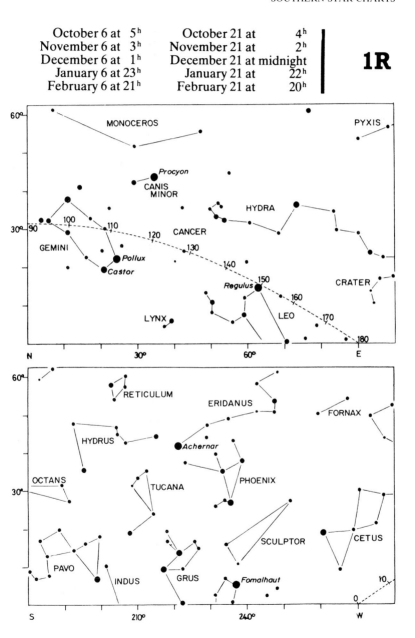

2L

November 6 at 5^h	November 21 at 4^h
December 6 at 3^h	December 21 at 2^h
January 6 at 1^h	January 21 at midnight
February 6 at 23^h	February 21 at 22^h
March 6 at 21^h	March 21 at 20^h

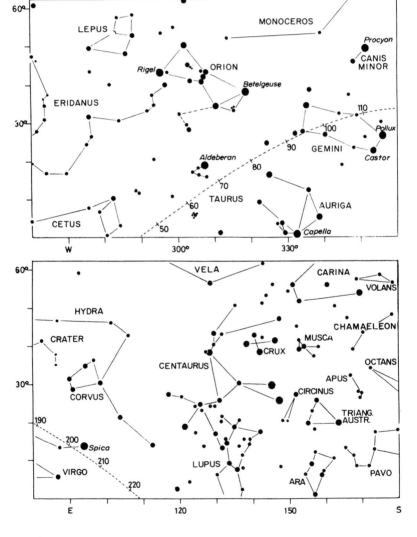

November 6 at	5ʰ	November 21 at	4ʰ
December 6 at	3ʰ	December 21 at	2ʰ
January 6 at	1ʰ	January 21 at midnight	
February 6 at 23ʰ		February 21 at	22ʰ
March 6 at 21ʰ		March 21 at	20ʰ

2R

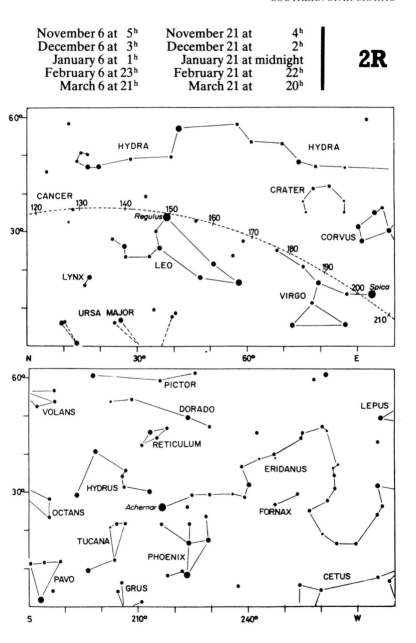

3L

January 6 at 3^h	January 21 at 2^h
February 6 at 1^h	February 21 at midnight
March 6 at 23^h	March 21 at 22^h
April 6 at 21^h	April 21 at 20^h
May 6 at 19^h	May 21 at 18^h

January 6 at 3^h	January 21 at 2^h
February 6 at 1^h	February 21 at midnight
March 6 at 23^h	March 21 at 22^h
April 6 at 21^h	April 21 at 20^h
May 6 at 19^h	May 21 at 18^h

3R

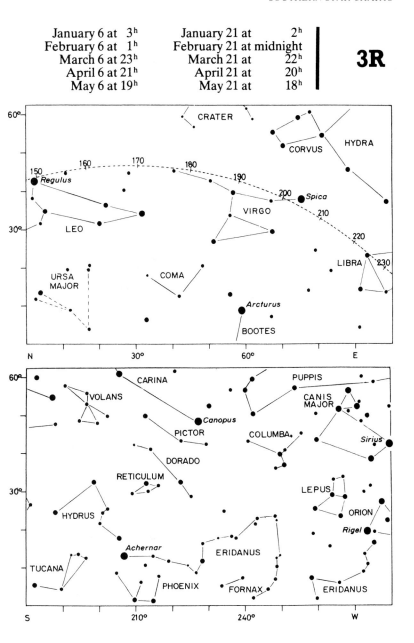

4L

February 6 at 3[h]	February 21 at 2[h]
March 6 at 1[h]	March 21 at midnight
April 6 at 23[h]	April 21 at 22[h]
May 6 at 21[h]	May 21 at 20[h]
June 6 at 19[h]	June 21 at 18[h]

February 6 at 3ʰ	February 21 at 2ʰ	
March 6 at 1ʰ	March 21 at midnight	**4R**
April 6 at 23ʰ	April 21 at 22ʰ	
May 6 at 21ʰ	May 21 at 20ʰ	
June 6 at 19ʰ	June 21 at 18ʰ	

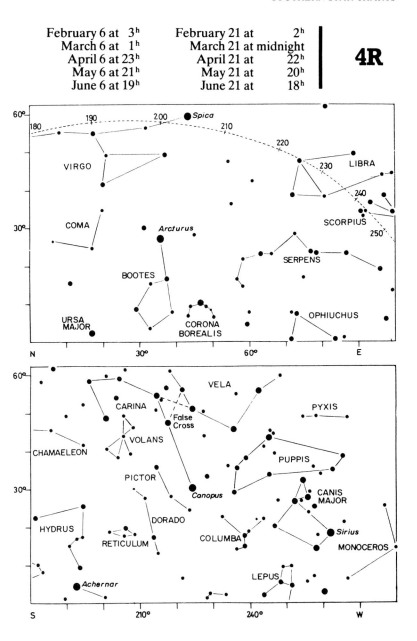

5L

March 6 at 3ʰ	March 21 at 2ʰ
April 6 at 1ʰ	April 21 at midnight
May 6 at 23ʰ	May 21 at 22ʰ
June 6 at 21ʰ	June 21 at 20ʰ
July 6 at 19ʰ	July 21 at 18ʰ

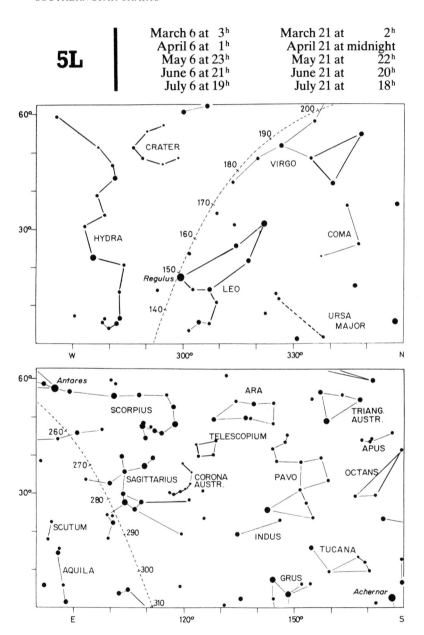

March 6 at 3ʰ	March 21 at 2ʰ
April 6 at 1ʰ	April 21 at midnight
May 6 at 23ʰ	May 21 at 22ʰ
June 6 at 21ʰ	June 21 at 20ʰ
July 6 at 19ʰ	July 21 at 18ʰ

5R

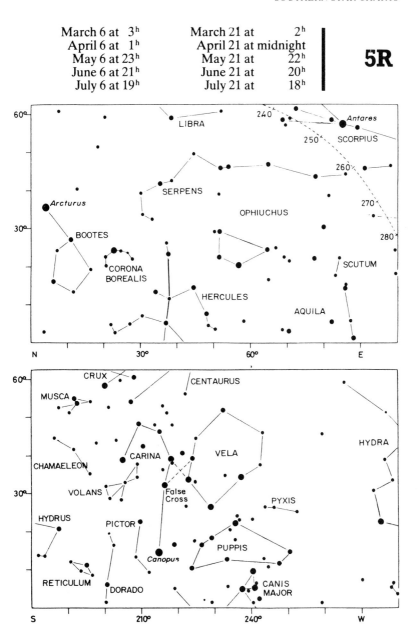

49

6L

March 6 at 5ʰ
April 6 at 3ʰ
May 6 at 1ʰ
June 6 at 23ʰ
July 6 at 21ʰ

March 21 at 4ʰ
April 21 at 2ʰ
May 21 at midnight
June 21 at 22ʰ
July 21 at 20ʰ

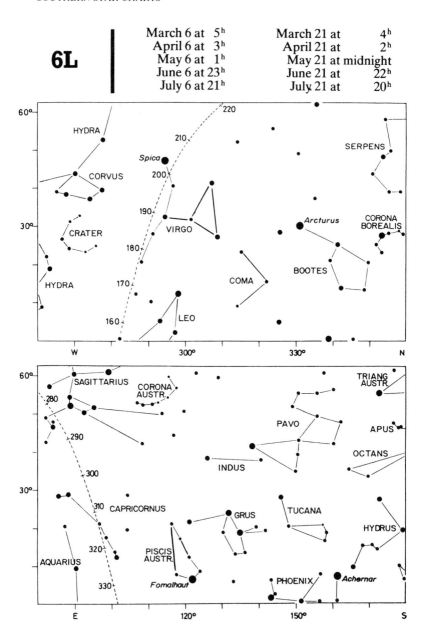

March 6 at 5ʰ   March 21 at   4ʰ
April 6 at 3ʰ   April 21 at   2ʰ
May 6 at 1ʰ   May 21 at midnight
June 6 at 23ʰ   June 21 at   22ʰ
July 6 at 21ʰ   July 21 at   20ʰ

6R

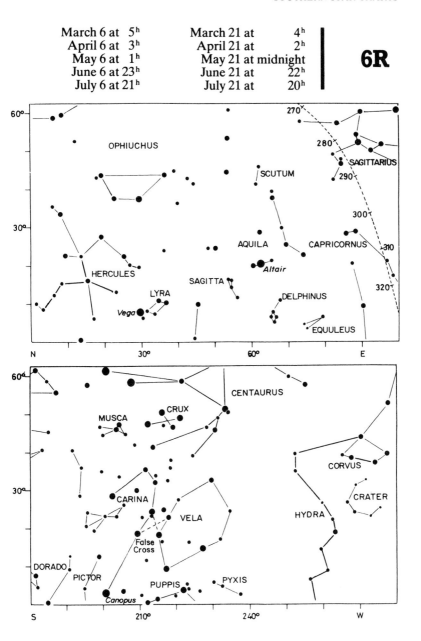

7L

April 6 at 5ʰ	April 21 at 4ʰ
May 6 at 3ʰ	May 21 at 2ʰ
June 6 at 1ʰ	June 21 at midnight
July 6 at 23ʰ	July 21 at 22ʰ
August 6 at 21ʰ	August 21 at 20ʰ

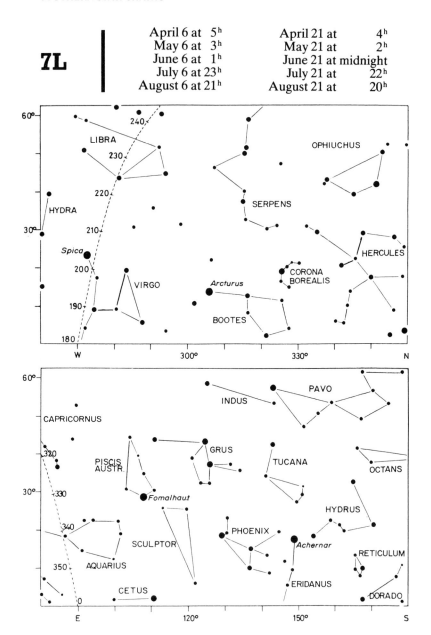

April 6 at 5ʰ   April 21 at 4ʰ
May 6 at 3ʰ   May 21 at 2ʰ
June 6 at 1ʰ   June 21 at midnight
July 6 at 23ʰ   July 21 at 22ʰ
August 6 at 21ʰ   August 21 at 20ʰ

7R

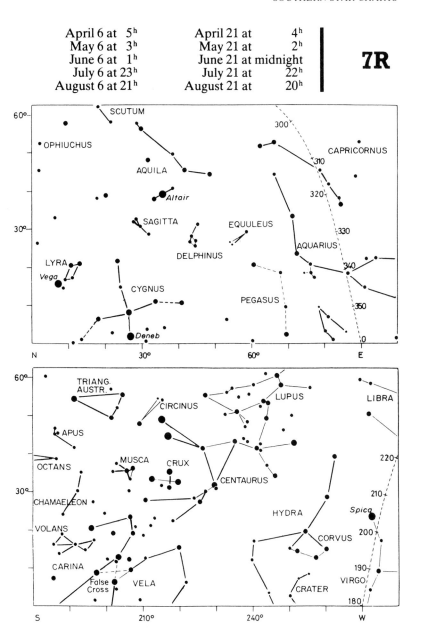

8L

May 6 at 5ʰ	May 21 at 4ʰ
June 6 at 3ʰ	June 21 at 2ʰ
July 6 at 1ʰ	July 21 at midnight
August 6 at 23ʰ	August 21 at 22ʰ
September 6 at 21ʰ	September 21 at 20ʰ

May 6 at 5ʰ	May 21 at 4ʰ	
June 6 at 3ʰ	June 21 at 2ʰ	
July 6 at 1ʰ	July 21 at midnight	**8R**
August 6 at 23ʰ	August 21 at 22ʰ	
September 6 at 21ʰ	September 21 at 20ʰ	

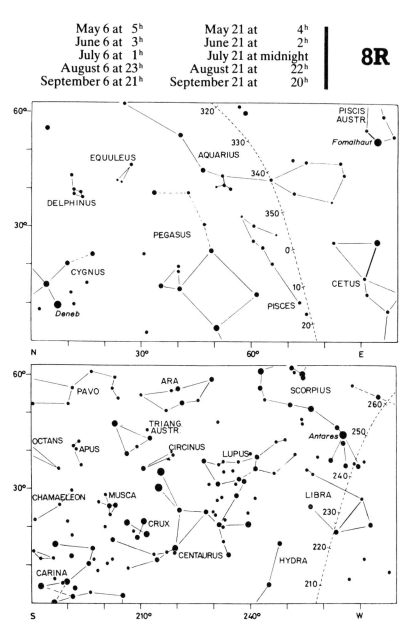

9L

June 6 at 5^h	June 21 at 4^h
July 6 at 3^h	July 21 at 2^h
August 6 at 1^h	August 21 at midnight
September 6 at 23^h	September 21 at 22^h
October 6 at 21^h	October 21 at 20^h

June 6 at 5ʰ   June 21 at   4ʰ
July 6 at 3ʰ   July 21 at   2ʰ
August 6 at 1ʰ   August 21 at midnight   **9R**
September 6 at 23ʰ   September 21 at   22ʰ
October 6 at 21ʰ   October 21 at   20ʰ

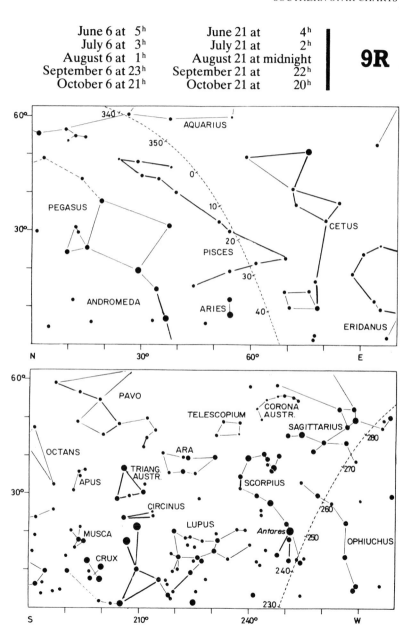

10L

July 6 at 5ʰ	July 21 at 4ʰ
August 6 at 3ʰ	August 21 at 2ʰ
September 6 at 1ʰ	September 21 at midnight
October 6 at 23ʰ	October 21 at 22ʰ
November 6 at 21ʰ	November 21 at 20ʰ

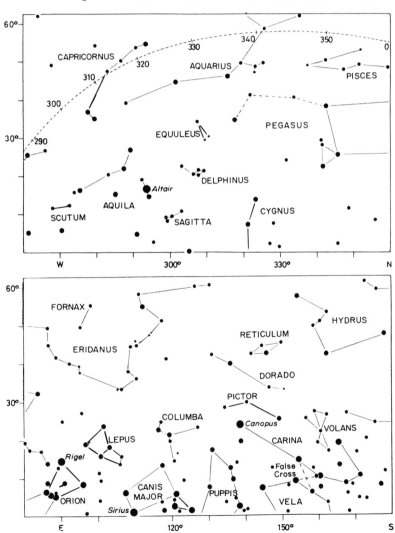

July 6 at 5ʰ	July 21 at 4ʰ	
August 6 at 3ʰ	August 21 at 2ʰ	
September 6 at 1ʰ	September 21 at midnight	**10R**
October 6 at 23ʰ	October 21 at 22ʰ	
November 6 at 21ʰ	November 21 at 20ʰ	

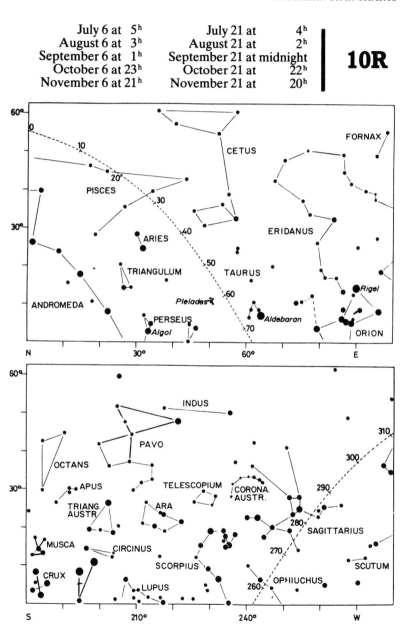

11L

August 6 at 5^h	August 21 at 4^h
September 6 at 3^h	September 21 at 2^h
October 6 at 1^h	October 21 at midnight
November 6 at 23^h	November 21 at 22^h
December 6 at 21^h	December 21 at 20^h

60°

CETUS

Fomalhaut

0   10

20

AQUARIUS   350

PISCES   30

340

CAPRICORNUS   330

320

30°

310

TRIANG.

PEGASUS

ANDROMEDA

EQUULEUS

W   300°   330°   N

60°

ERIDANUS   RETICULUM

DORADO   HYDRUS

PICTOR

LEPUS   COLUMBA

Canopus

VOLANS

CARINA   CHAMAELEON

30°

Sirius

CANIS
MAJOR   PUPPIS

MUSCA

MONOCEROS   CRUX

VELA

PYXIS

Procyon

E   120°   150°   S

August 6 at 5ʰ	August 21 at 4ʰ	
September 6 at 3ʰ	September 21 at 2ʰ	**11R**
October 6 at 1ʰ	October 21 at midnight	
November 6 at 23ʰ	November 21 at 22ʰ	
December 6 at 21ʰ	December 21 at 20ʰ	

September 6 at 5^h	September 21 at 4^h
October 6 at 3^h	October 21 at 2^h
November 6 at 1^h	November 21 at midnight
December 6 at 23^h	December 21 at 22^h
January 6 at 21^h	January 21 at 20^h

12L

September 6 at 5^h	September 21 at 4^h	
October 6 at 3^h	October 21 at 2^h	**12R**
November 6 at 1^h	November 21 at midnight	
December 6 at 23^h	December 21 at 22^h	
January 6 at 21^h	January 21 at 20^h	

ERIDANUS — Rigel — ORION — Betelgeuse — Aldebaran — TAURUS — AURIGA — Capella — GEMINI — Castor — Pollux — CANIS MINOR — Procyon — Sirius — CANIS MAJOR — MONOCEROS — PUPPIS — HYDRA

70 80 90 100 110 120 130

60° 30° N 30° 60° E

HYDRUS — Achernar — PHOENIX — TUCANA — SCULPTOR — OCTANS — GRUS — Fomalhaut — APUS — PAVO — INDUS — PISCIS AUSTR. — AQUARIUS — ARA — CAPRICORNUS

350 340 330 320

60° 30° S 210° 240° W

63

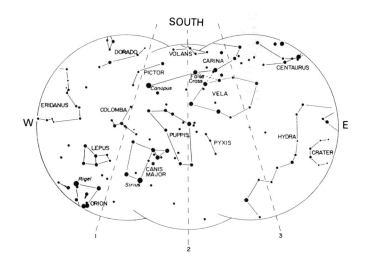

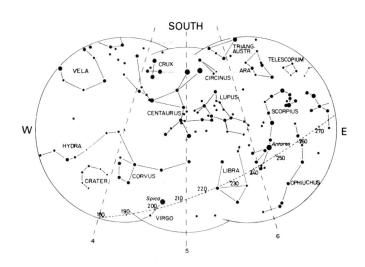

Southern Hemisphere Overhead Stars

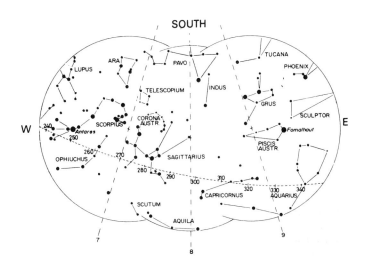

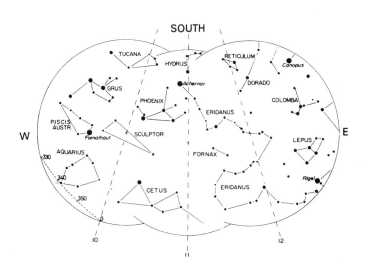

Southern Hemisphere Overhead Stars

The Planets and the Ecliptic

The paths of the planets about the Sun all lie close to the plane of the ecliptic, which is marked for us in the sky by the apparent path of the Sun among the stars, and is shown on the star charts by a broken line. The Moon and planets will always be found close to this line, never departing from it by more than about 7 degrees. Thus the planets are most favourably placed for observation when the ecliptic is well displayed, and this means that it should be as high in the sky as possible. This avoids the difficulty of finding a clear horizon, and also overcomes the problem of atmospheric absorption, which greatly reduces the light of the stars. Thus a star at an altitude of 10 degrees suffers a loss of 60 per cent of its light, which corresponds to a whole magnitude; at an altitude of only 4 degrees, the loss may amount to two magnitudes.

The position of the ecliptic in the sky is therefore of great importance, and since it is tilted at about 23½ degrees to the Equator, it is only at certain times of the day or year that it is displayed to the best advantage. It will be realized that the Sun (and therefore the ecliptic) is at its highest in the sky at noon in mid-summer, and at its lowest at noon in midwinter. Allowing for the daily motion of the sky, these times lead to the fact that the ecliptic is highest at midnight in winter, at sunset in the spring, at noon in summer and at sunrise in the autumn. Hence these are the best times to see the planets. Thus, if Venus is an evening object in the western sky after sunset, it will be seen to best advantage if this occurs in the spring, when the ecliptic is high in the sky and slopes down steeply to the horizon. This means that the planet is not only higher in the sky, but will remain for a much longer period above the horizon. For similar reasons, a morning object will be seen at its best on autumn mornings before sunrise, when the ecliptic is high in the east. The outer planets, which can come to opposition (i.e. opposite the Sun), are best seen when opposition occurs in the winter months, when the ecliptic is high in the sky at midnight.

The seasons are reversed in the Southern Hemisphere, spring beginning at the September Equinox, when the Sun crosses the Equator on its way south, summer beginning at the December

Solstice, when the Sun is highest in the southern sky, and so on. Thus, the times when the ecliptic is highest in the sky, and therefore best placed for observing the planets, may be summarized as follows:

	Midnight	*Sunrise*	*Noon*	*Sunset*
Northern lats.	December	September	June	March
Southern lats.	June	March	December	September

In addition to the daily rotation of the celestial sphere from east to west, the planets have a motion of their own among the stars. The apparent movement is generally *direct*, i.e. to the east, in the direction of increasing longitude, but for a certain period (which depends on the distance of the planet) this apparent motion is reversed. With the outer planets this *retrograde* motion occurs about the time of opposition. Owing to the different inclination of the orbits of these planets, the actual effect is to cause the apparent path to form a loop, or sometimes an S-shaped curve. The same effect is present in the motion of the inferior planets, Mercury and Venus, but it is not so obvious, since it always occurs at the time of inferior conjunction.

The inferior planets, Mercury and Venus, move in smaller orbits than that of the Earth, and so are always seen near the Sun. They are most obvious at the times of greatest angular distance from the Sun (greatest elongation), which may reach 28 degrees for Mercury, or 47 degrees for Venus. They are seen as evening objects in the western sky after sunset (at eastern elongations) or as morning objects in the eastern sky before sunrise (at western elongations). The succession of phenomena, conjunctions and elongations always follows the same order, but the intervals between them are not equal. Thus, if either planet is moving round the far side of its orbit its motion will be to the east, in the same direction in which the Sun appears to be moving. It therefore takes much longer for the planet to overtake the Sun – that is, to come to superior conjunction – than it does when moving round to inferior conjunction, between Sun and Earth. The intervals given in the following table are average values; they remain fairly constant in the case of Venus, which travels in an almost circular orbit. In the case of Mercury, however, conditions vary widely because of the great eccentricity and inclination of the planet's orbit.

		Mercury	*Venus*
Inferior conj.	to Elongation West	22 days	72 days
Elongation West	to Superior conj.	36 days	220 days
Superior conj.	to Elongation East	36 days	220 days
Elongation East	to Inferior conj.	22 days	72 days

The greatest brilliancy of Venus always occurs about 36 days before or after inferior conjunction. This will be about a month *after* greatest eastern elongation (as an evening object), or a month *before* greatest western elongation (as a morning object). No such rule can be given for Mercury, because its distance from the Earth and the Sun can vary over a wide range.

Mercury is not likely to be seen unless a clear horizon is available. It is seldom seen as much as 10 degrees above the horizon in the twilight sky in northern latitudes, but this figure is often exceeded in the Southern Hemisphere. This favourable condition arises because the maximum elongation of 28 degrees can occur only when the planet is at aphelion (farthest from the Sun), and this point lies well south of the Equator. Northern observers must be content with smaller elongations, which may be as little as 18 degrees at perihelion. In general, it may be said that the most favourable times for seeing Mercury as an evening object will be in spring, some days before greatest eastern elongation; in autumn, it may be seen as a morning object some days after greatest western elongation.

Venus is the brightest of the planets and may be seen on occasions in broad daylight. Like Mercury, it is alternately a morning and an evening object, and it will be highest in the sky when it is a morning object in autumn, or an evening object in spring. The phenomena of Venus given in the table above can occur only in the months of January, April, June, August and November, and it will be realized that they do not all lead to favourable apparitions of the planet. In fact, Venus is to be seen at its best as an evening object in northern latitudes when eastern elongation occurs in June. The planet is then well north of the Sun in the preceding spring months, and is a brilliant object in the evening sky over a long period. In the Southern Hemisphere a November elongation is best. For similar reasons, Venus gives a prolonged display as a morning object in the months following western elongation in November (in northern latitudes) or in June (in the Southern Hemisphere).

The superior planets, which travel in orbits larger than that of the Earth, differ from Mercury and Venus in that they can be seen opposite the Sun in the sky. The superior planets are morning objects after conjunction with the Sun, rising earlier each day until they come to opposition. They will then be nearest to the Earth (and therefore at their brightest), and will then be on the meridian at midnight, due south in northern latitudes, but due north in the Southern Hemisphere. After opposition they are evening objects, setting earlier each evening until they set in the west with the Sun at the next conjunction. The change in brightness about the time of opposition is most noticeable in the case of Mars, whose distance from Earth can vary considerably and rapidly. The other superior planets are at such great distances that there is very little change in brightness from one opposition to another. The effect of altitude is, however, of some importance, for at a December opposition in northern latitudes the planets will be among the stars of Taurus or Gemini, and can then be at an altitude of more than 60 degrees in southern England. At a summer opposition, when the planet is in Sagittarius, it may only rise to about 15 degrees above the southern horizon, and so makes a less impressive appearance. In the Southern Hemisphere, the reverse conditions apply, a June opposition being the best, with the planet in Sagittarius at an altitude which can reach 80 degrees above the northern horizon for observers in South Africa.

Mars, whose orbit is appreciably eccentric, comes nearest to the Earth at an opposition at the end of August. It may then be brighter even than Jupiter, but rather low in the sky in Aquarius for northern observers, though very well placed for those in southern latitudes. These favourable oppositions occur every fifteen or seventeen years (1956, 1971, 1988, 2003) but in the Northern Hemisphere the planet is probably better seen at an opposition in the autumn or winter months, when it is higher in the sky. Oppositions of Mars occur at an average interval of 780 days, and during this time the planet makes a complete circuit of the sky.

Jupiter is always a bright planet, and comes to opposition a month later each year, having moved, roughly speaking, from one Zodiacal constellation to the next.

Saturn moves much more slowly than Jupiter, and may remain in the same constellation for several years. The brightness of Saturn depends on the aspects of its rings, as well as on the distance from Earth and Sun. The rings were inclined towards the Earth and Sun in 1980 and are now past their maximum opening. The next passage of both Earth and Sun through the ring-plane will not occur until 1995.

Uranus, *Neptune*, and *Pluto* are hardly likely to attract the attention of observers without adequate instruments.

Phases of the Moon, 1995

New Moon			*First Quarter*			*Full Moon*			*Last Quarter*		
	d	h m		d	h m		d	h m		d	h m
Jan.	1	10 56	Jan.	8	15 46	Jan.	16	20 26	Jan.	24	04 58
Jan.	30	22 48	Feb.	7	12 54	Feb.	15	12 15	Feb.	22	13 04
Mar.	1	11 48	Mar.	9	10 14	Mar.	17	01 26	Mar.	23	20 10
Mar.	31	02 09	Apr.	8	05 35	Apr.	15	12 08	Apr.	22	03 18
Apr.	29	17 36	May	7	21 44	May	14	20 48	May	21	11 36
May	29	09 27	June	6	10 26	June	13	04 03	June	19	22 01
June	28	00 50	July	5	20 02	July	12	10 49	July	19	11 10
July	27	15 13	Aug.	4	03 16	Aug.	10	18 16	Aug.	18	03 04
Aug.	26	04 31	Sept.	2	09 03	Sept.	9	03 37	Sept.	16	21 09
Sept.	24	16 55	Oct.	1	14 36	Oct.	8	15 52	Oct.	16	16 26
Oct.	24	04 36	Oct.	30	21 17	Nov.	7	07 21	Nov.	15	11 40
Nov.	22	15 43	Nov.	29	06 28	Dec.	7	01 27	Dec.	15	05 31
Dec.	22	02 22	Dec.	28	19 06						

All times are GMT.

Longitudes of the Sun, Moon and Planets in 1995

DATE		Sun	Moon	Venus	Mars	Jupiter	Saturn
		°	°	°	°	°	°
January	6	285	345	239	153	246	338
	21	300	170	253	151	248	340
February	6	317	30	271	145	251	342
	21	332	222	288	140	253	343
March	6	345	38	304	135	254	345
	21	0	232	321	133	255	347
April	6	16	81	341	134	255	349
	21	30	286	358	137	255	350
May	6	45	113	17	142	254	352
	21	59	323	34	148	252	353
June	6	75	160	54	155	250	354
	21	89	12	72	163	248	355
July	6	103	196	91	171	247	355
	21	118	45	109	179	246	355
August	6	133	248	129	189	246	354
	21	147	89	147	198	246	353
September	6	163	301	167	209	247	352
	21	178	133	185	219	249	351
October	6	192	339	205	229	251	350
	21	207	167	223	240	254	349
November	6	223	28	243	252	257	348
	21	238	216	261	262	260	348
December	6	253	62	280	274	264	348
	21	269	253	298	285	267	349

Longitude of *Uranus* 298°
            Neptune 294°

Moon: Longitude of ascending node
        Jan. 1: 221°   Dec. 31: 202°

Mercury moves so quickly among the stars that it is not possible to indicate its position on the star charts at a convenient interval. The monthly notes must be consulted for the best times at which the planet may be seen.

The positions of the other planets are given in the table on the previous page. This gives the apparent longitudes on dates which correspond to those of the star charts, and the position of the planet may at once be found near the ecliptic at the given longitude.

Examples
In the Southern Hemisphere two planets are seen in the eastern morning sky in early January. Identify them.

> The Southern Star Chart 3L shows the eastern sky at January 6^d 03^h and shows longitudes 210°–255°. Reference to the table on page 71 gives the longitude of Venus as 239° and that of Jupiter as 246°. Thus these planets are to be found in the eastern sky and the one lower down is Jupiter.

The positions of the Sun and Moon can be plotted on the star maps in the same manner as for the planets. The average daily motion of the Sun is 1°, and of the Moon 13°. For the Moon an indication of its position relative to the ecliptic may be obtained from a considera-tion of its longitude relative to that of the ascending node. The latter changes only slowly during the year as will be seen from the values given on the previous page. Let us call the difference in longitude of Moon-node, d. Then if d = 0°, 180° or 360° the Moon is on the ecliptic. If d = 90° the Moon is 5° north of the ecliptic and if d = 270° the Moon is 5° south of the ecliptic.

On May 6 the Moon's longitude is given as 113° and the longitude of the node is found by interpolation to be about 214°. Thus d = 259° and the Moon is about 5° south of the ecliptic. Its position may be plotted on Northern Star Charts 1L, 2R, 3R, 4L, 4R, 5L, 11R, 12L and Southern Star Charts 1R, 2L, 3L, 4L, 12R.

Events in 1995

ECLIPSES

There will be three eclipses, two of the Sun and one of the Moon.

April 15: partial eclipse of the Moon – America, Australasia, Asia.

April 29: annular eclipse of the Sun – America (not North), West Africa.

October 24: total eclipse of the Sun – Arabia, Asia, Australia.

THE PLANETS

Mercury may be seen more easily from northern latitudes in the evenings about the time of greatest eastern elongation (May 12) and in the mornings around greatest western elongation (October 20). In the Southern Hemisphere the dates are March 1 (morning) and September 9 (evening).

Venus is visible in the mornings until July. From October onwards it is visible in the evenings.

Mars is at opposition on February 12.

Jupiter is at opposition on June 1.

Saturn is at opposition on September 14.

Uranus is at opposition on July 21.

Neptune is at opposition on July 17.

Pluto is at opposition on May 20.

JANUARY

New Moon: January 1, 30   *Full Moon:* January 16

EARTH is at perihelion (nearest to the Sun) on January 4 at a distance of 147 million kilometres.

MERCURY is at greatest eastern elongation on January 19 (19°) and after the first ten days of the month may be seen by Northern Hemisphere observers low in the south-western sky after sunset. Observers in the Southern Hemisphere will be able to locate it a few days earlier and enjoy a period of visibility of about three weeks. During this period of visibility the magnitude of Mercury fades from −0.8 to +0.9.

VENUS is a morning object and will reach greatest western elongation (47°) on January 13. At this time a telescope will show the planet to be half illuminated like the Moon at Last Quarter. Because of its southern declination, observers in the British Isles will never see it high in the sky: nevertheless it will be visible in the south-eastern sky for several hours before dawn, a very bright object at magnitude −4.4, brighter than it will be at any time during the remainder of the year. Venus passes 3° North of Jupiter on January 14.

MARS is becoming visible in the eastern sky in the evenings and for observers in the British Isles it will be visible low in the eastern sky as soon as the sky is really dark, by the end of the month. During January its magnitude brightens from −0.4 to −1.0. Mars is moving slowly retrograde in Leo, passing several degrees north of Regulus towards the end of January. The path of Mars among the stars from January to September is shown in Figure 1.

JUPITER, magnitude −1.8, is a brilliant object in the mornings, visible low in the south-eastern sky before sunrise. Its path among the stars is shown in Figure 7, given with the notes for June. On January 14 Venus passes 3° N. of Jupiter.

SATURN, magnitude +1.0, is an evening object and may be seen in the south-western sky in Aquarius. The path of Saturn among the stars is shown in Figure 10, given with the notes for September.

THE FIRST-MAGNITUDE STARS. Conventionally, the twenty-one brightest stars in the sky are classed as being of the first magnitude; they range from Sirius (−1.46) down to Regulus (+1.35). Next in order comes Adhara (Epsilon Canis Majoris), which is of magnitude 1.50 and is not reckoned among the élite; neither is Castor, the senior but fainter of the Twins, at magnitude 1.58.

Many of the first-magnitude stars are sufficiently close to the Equator to be seen from every inhabited country, but there are some which are not, and it may be interesting to list those which are at declinations of 40° or higher. There are only two in the far north

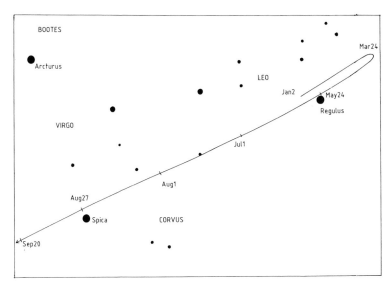

Figure 1. The path of Mars in 1995.

(Vega, at declination +39°, just missed) but no less than six in the far south:

(North)	Deneb, +45°
	Capella, +40°
(South)	Acrux, −63°
	Alpha Centauri, −61°
	Agena, −60°
	Beta Crucis, −60°
	Achernar, −57°
	Canopus, −53°

All these far-southern stars are invisible from Britain; go to the southern part of New Zealand, and you will lose Deneb and Capella (as well as Vega).

To find your limiting declination, simply take your latitude on the Earth's surface and subtract it from 90 degrees. This gives your co-latitude. The latitude of Athens, for example, is 38°N. 90 − 38 = 52; therefore any star south of latitude −52° will never rise, and any star north of +52° will never set. Thus you will never see Canopus, but Dubhe in the Great Bear, declination +62°, will be circumpolar. Falkland Islanders (latitude −51°) will see Canopus all the time, but Capella never.

The southernmost of the first-magnitude stars available from England is Fomalhaut (declination −30°). During January evenings Capella is near the zenith or overhead point from Britain, but rather low down from countries such as Australia and South Africa. From London it is just circumpolar, though on summer evenings it skims the horizon, so that any mist or light pollution will hide it.

EARTH AT PERIHELION. On January 4 the Earth is at its closest to the Sun, at 147 million kilometres or 91.4 million miles. At aphelion, in July, the distance will be 152 million kilometres or 94.5 million miles. The difference therefore amounts to approximately 5 million kilometres or 3 million miles, which is not very much; the Earth's orbit is not far from circular. It is worth looking at the distance-ranges of the other planets:

	Range in millions of		*Orbital Eccentricity*
	km	*miles*	
Mercury	24	15	0.206
Venus	1.4	0.9	0.007
Earth	5	3	0.017
Mars	42	26	0.093
Jupiter	75	47	0.048
Saturn	160	99	0.056
Uranus	269	167	0.047
Neptune	81	50	0.009
Pluto	2950	1833	0.248

Obviously Pluto is the planet with the greatest range – but can we class Pluto as a proper planet at all? It seems to be more in the nature of a planetesimal. Of the bona-fide planets, Venus and Neptune have the least orbital eccentricities.

The fact that Mars has an orbit more eccentric than ours means that its opposition magnitude can vary considerably. At its best it may outshine every planet apart from Venus, as it will next do in 2003; at the least favourable oppositions the magnitude remains below −1, so that it cannot even match Sirius. When furthest from us, Mars is not much brighter than the Pole Star.

FEBRUARY

Full Moon: February 15

MERCURY is at inferior conjunction on February 3 and reaches greatest western elongation on March 1. During this period it is well south of the Sun and thus poorly placed for observation by those in northern temperate latitudes. However, the planet is well placed for observation by those in the Southern Hemisphere. For observers in southern latitudes this will be the most favourable morning apparition of the year. Figure 2 shows, for observers in latitudes S.35°, the changes in azimuth (true bearing from the north through east, south, and west) and altitude of Mercury on successive evenings when the Sun is 6° below the horizon. This condition is known as the beginning of morning civil twilight and in this latitude and at this time of year occurs about 30 minutes before sunrise. The changes in the brightness of the planet are indicated by the relative sizes of the circles marking Mercury's position at five-day intervals. It will be noticed that Mercury is at its brightest after it reaches greatest western elongation (27°) on March 1.

VENUS, magnitude −4.2, continues to be visible as a brilliant object in the south-eastern sky for a considerable time before dawn.

MARS is at opposition on February 12 which means that it is visible throughout the hours of darkness, rising in the east at sunset and setting in the west at sunrise. Mars has a slightly reddish tint which is an aid to identification. Its magnitude is −1.2, about as faint as it can be at opposition. This is because Mars is at aphelion next month and the minimum distance of Mars from the Earth, on February 11, is 101 million kilometres. When opposition occurs near perihelion Mars is 1½ magnitudes brighter!

JUPITER is a brilliant morning object, low in the south-eastern sky for several hours before dawn. Jupiter has a magnitude of −2.0.

.

SATURN, magnitude +1.0, is coming to the end of its period of visibility and is only visible for a short while low in the west-south-western sky in the early evening. By the middle of the month it will be lost to view in the gathering twilight.

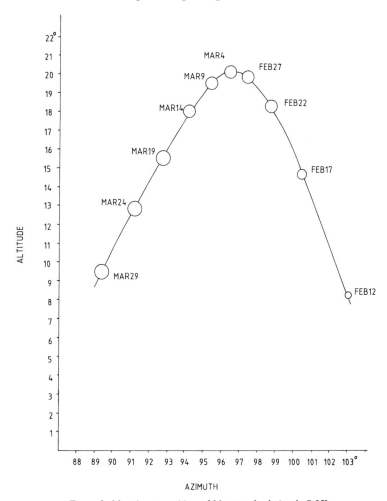

Figure 2. Morning apparition of Mercury for latitutde S.35°.

THE CELESTIAL TWINS. Gemini, the Twins, is one of the largest and most imposing of the Zodiacal constellations. In mythology, Castor and Pollux were twin boys, but Pollux was immortal, while Castor was not. When Castor was killed in battle, Pollux pleaded to be allowed to share his immortality with his brother; his wish was granted, and both were placed in the sky.

Though Castor is the 'senior twin', and was ranked by some early astronomers as the brighter of the two, it is now the fainter by half a magnitude, and the difference is obvious at a glance. The colours, too, are different; Castor is white, while Pollux is an orange star of spectral type K. Moreover, Pollux is single, while Castor is multiple. A moderate telescope will show the two main components, each is a spectroscopic binary, and there is a third, faint member of the group (Castor C or YY Geminorum) which is a spectroscopic binary. Castor therefore consists of six stars, four bright and two dim.

Though they appear side by side in the sky, they are not true neighbours; Pollux is 36 light-years away from us, Castor 46. Pollux has a luminosity 60 times that of the Sun, and its orange hue is evident even with the naked eye; binoculars bring it out well.

The third star of Gemini is Gamma or Alhena, magnitude 1.9, which lies around midway between Pollux and Betelgeux in Orion. It is a white star, equal to more than 80 Suns.

There are two notable variable stars in Gemini. Zeta (Mekbuda) is a typical Cepheid, with a range of from magnitude 3.7 to 4.1 and a period of 10.15 days; a good comparison star is the nearby Lambda (3.6), while Delta (3.5) can also be used. Eta Geminorum (Propus) is of different type. The range is from 3.2 to 3.9, and the period is around 233 days; the period and range are not constant – Eta is classed as a semi-regular star. The light curve is complicated by the fact that there is another member of the system which can eclipse the main system – and there is a binary companion of magnitude 8.8, which has a separation of 1.4 from the main star. The revolution period is 474 years.

Like many semi-regular variables, Eta is reddish, and of type M; it is 186 light-years away, and over 130 times as luminous as the Sun. A good comparison star when Eta is bright is Mu (Tejat), magnitude 2.9 and also of type M; when Eta is near minimum, use Nu (4.1) and l (4.2).

In this area lies M.35, a beautiful open cluster. It was discovered by de Chéseaux in 1746, and is visible with the naked eye; a small

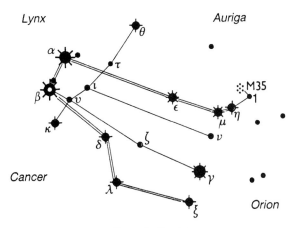

Figure 3. Gemini.

telescope will resolve it into stars. The distance is over 2800 light-years, and the true diameter may be as much as 30 light-years.

The Milky Way flows through Gemini, and the whole area is very rich. It is co-incidental that two planets were discovered in this constellation; Uranus by William Herschel in 1781, and Pluto by Clyde Tombaugh in 1930.

MARCH

New Moon: March 1, 31   *Full Moon:* March 17

Equinox: March 21

Summer Time in Great Britain and Northern Ireland commences on
March 26.

MERCURY, being at greatest western elongation (27°) on the first
day of the month is still well placed for observation by observers in
the Southern Hemisphere for all except the last days of the month
and they should refer to Figure 2 in the notes for February. For
observers in northern temperate latitudes Mercury remains unsuitably placed for observation.

VENUS is still a brilliant morning object, magnitude −4.0. It is
well south of the Equator so that observers in southern latitudes are
able to see the planet for around three hours before dawn – about
three times as long as for those in the latitudes of the British
Isles.

MARS, although not long past opposition, is fading in brightness
and by the end of March it is a whole magnitude fainter than when it
was at opposition. Mars is visible for the greater part of the night,
being well above the eastern horizon as soon as it is dark enough to
be visible. Mars is moving retrograde in Cancer until it reaches its
second stationary point on March 24.

JUPITER, magnitude −2.2, continues to be visible as a brilliant
morning object in the south-eastern skies before sunrise. Its
declination is −22° so that observers in the British Isles will only see
it at altitudes less than about 17°, even at transit.

SATURN is at conjunction on March 6 and is therefore unsuitably
placed for observation during the month.

VESTA. Vesta, the brightest member of the asteroid swarm, is on view this month, not far from the third-magnitude star Zeta Tauri. Its magnitude is just above 8; at its best it can just achieve naked-eye visibility – the only asteroid to do so. It was the fourth in order of discovery, and was first identified by Olbers on March 29, 1807; the only asteroids previously known were Ceres, Pallas, and Juno.

Ceres, with a diameter of 584 miles, is much the largest of the asteroids. Vesta – 358 miles – comes second. This honour was formerly afforded to Pallas, and it is true that Pallas' longest diameter is 360 miles; but unlike Vesta it is not a true sphere, and the shortest diameter is no more than 292 miles.

Vesta is quite unlike the other major members of the swarm. It seems that its surface is covered with volcanic rock which was once molten; the albedo is 0.3, as against only 0.05 for Ceres. The distance from the Sun ranges between 200 million and 220 million miles, and the period is 3.63 years; the axial rotation amounts to 5.34 hours.

Fortunately, Vesta makes frequent close approaches to another asteroid, 197 Arete, and this has enabled its mass to be measured fairly accurately; it amounts to 2.75×10^{23} gr., with a density of 3.1 gr/cm^3. Ceres, Pallas, and Vesta combined make up 55 per cent of the total mass of the asteroids.

Powerful telescopes will show that Vesta is unstellar, but no surface details have been made out, though slight changes in brightness due to the axial rotation indicate that the surface is not uniform. There have been suggestions that Vesta is the source of the eucrite meteorites, though this is little more than conjecture.

TRANSFERRED STAR! Taurus, the Bull, adjoins Gemini, and at present Vesta lies not far from the boundary of the two constellations. Zeta Tauri (sometimes still known by its old name of Alheka) is of magnitude 3.0, and is well over a thousand times as powerful as the Sun; the distance is nearly 500 light-years. Close beside it is the famous Crab Nebula (Messier 1), remnant of the supernova seen in 1054; the Crab is just visible with powerful binoculars as a faint patch of light.

Beta Tauri, or Al Nath, is of magnitude 1.6. It was once included in Auriga, and was known as Gamma Aurigæ, though for some unknown reason it has been transferred to Taurus – even though it seems more logically to belong to the Auriga pattern. This is one of a few cases of transferred stars (for instance, Sigma Libræ was once

Gamma Scorpii). Taurus is, of course, most celebrated because it includes the Pleiades and the Hyades, the two most famous open clusters in the entire sky.

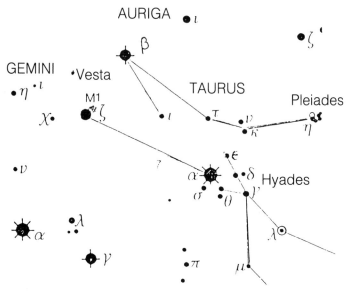

Figure 4. Vesta and Taurus.

APRIL

New Moon: April 29   *Full Moon:* April 15

MERCURY passes through superior conjunction on April 14 and it is only for about the last five days of the month, as it moves east of the Sun, that it is possible to observe it in the evening sky. Its magnitude is −1. Being well north of the Sun it is observers in the Northern Hemisphere who will get the best view. Indeed, this evening apparition, which spreads into the first three weeks of May, is the most suitable one of the year for observers in northern temperate latitudes. Figure 5 shows, for observers in latitude N.52°, the changes in azimuth (true bearing from the north through east, south, and west) and altitude of Mercury on successive evenings when the Sun is 6° below the horizon. This condition is known as the end of evening civil twilight and in this latitude and at this time of year occurs about 35 minutes after sunset. The changes in the brightness of the planet are indicated by the relative sizes of the circles marking Mercury's position at five-day intervals. It will be noticed that Mercury is at its brightest before it reaches greatest eastern elongation (22°) on May 12.

VENUS, magnitude −3.9, continues to be visible as a brilliant morning object. For observers in the Southern Hemisphere it is rising later each morning. For observers in the Northern Hemisphere it is rising earlier each morning, but so is the Sun, so that the actual interval of time between the rising of the two bodies (about an hour at the beginning of the month for observers in the British Isles) actually decreases very slowly during April.

MARS continues to be visible as an evening object. Its direct motion carries it from Cancer into Leo during the month. It has a magnitude of about +0.2.

JUPITER, magnitude −2.4, reaches its first stationary point on April 1, in Ophiuchus (see Figure 7 given with the notes for June). It is still a morning object and even for observers in northern temperate latitudes it is well clear of the south-eastern horizon before midnight, by the end of the month.

SATURN becomes visible as a difficult morning object, magnitude +1.2, early in the month, low above the eastern horizon before twilight inhibits observation. However, observers in the British Isles will have to wait until next month before they can glimpse the planet.

THE RETURN OF A COMET. Many periodical comets are known, but very few attain naked-eye visibility, and only one (Halley's) ever becomes really bright. One famous but dim wanderer is due to return this month: Comet de Vico–Swift.

It was originally found on August 23, 1844 by the Italian astronomer de Vico, and later in the year it reached magnitude 5, so that it was detectable without optical aid. There was even a short tail. The period was calculated to be 5.3 years, but future returns were unobserved, and the comet was given up as lost. Then, in 1894, the famous American comet-hunter Swift found a 13th-magnitude comet with a short tail, which also 'went missing'. In 1963, as a result

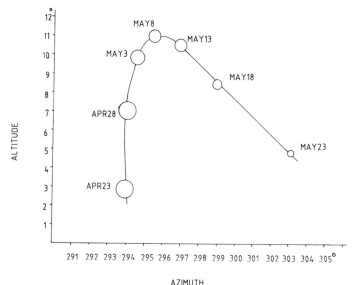

Figure 5. Evening apparition of Mercury for latitude N.52°.

of calculations by Brian Marsden, it was shown that the comets of de Vico and Swift were identical, and on June 30, 1965 it was recovered by Arnold Klemola in Argentina – though the magnitude was only 17.

There is every hope of its recovery at the present return, but it will certainly not become noticeable; its orbit is often altered by close approaches to Jupiter. Like so many comets, its wanderings are decidedly erratic.

OPHIUCHUS – IN THE ZODIAC! It is usually said that there are only twelve constellations in the Zodiac, but a thirteenth – Ophiuchus,

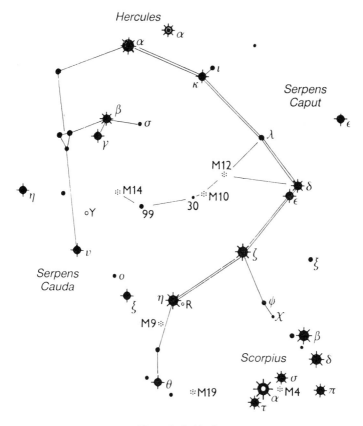

Figure 6. Ophiuchus.

the Serpent-bearer – does intrude into the Zodiacal band, between Scorpius and Sagittarius. Ophiuchus, once known as Serpentarius, is named in honour of Æsculapius, the mythological doctor – and in the sky is engaged in a struggle with Serpens, the Serpent, which has been pulled in half (Figure 6).

Ophiuchus is a very large constellation; the brightest star, Alpha (Rasalhague) is more than 12° north of the celestial Equator, while Theta (magnitude 3.3) is almost 25° south. An appreciable part of the Zodiac passes through the constellation, so that planets may enter it – as Jupiter does this month. The intrusion of Ophiuchus is a constant source of irritation to astrologers, who frankly do not know what to do about it!

There is no really well-marked pattern to the constellation, but it is notable as being exceptionally rich in globular clusters, no less than seven of which are included in Messier's catalogue.

THIS MONTH'S CENTENARY. April 22 is the centenary of the death of a well-known French astronomer, Étienne Léopold Trouvelot. He was born at Guyencourt on December 26, 1826, and educated in France, but emigrated to America in 1858 and became an assistant at the Harvard Observatory, where he carried out valuable work; he specialized in observing the planets (particularly Mars) and in solar prominences. Later he returned to his native country, and became assistant to Jules Janssen at the Meudon Observatory, Paris, where he remained for the rest of his life.

THIS MONTH'S ECLIPSES. On April 29 there will be an annular eclipse of the Sun; the track passes over the South Pacific, Peru, and the South Atlantic, but nothing will be seen from Europe. On April 15 there is a partial eclipse of the Moon; the time of mid-eclipse is 12ʰ 19ᵐ GMT, and the total obscuration is only 11 per cent.

MAY

New Moon: May 29   *Full Moon:* May 14

MERCURY is at greatest eastern elongation (22°) on May 12 and is therefore visible in the evening skies, as shown in Figure 5, given with the notes for April. Mercury is particularly well placed for observation by Northern Hemisphere observers, and from the latitudes of the British Isles it is visible for all except the last ten days of the month, low above the west-north-west horizon. During this period the magnitude of Mercury fades from −0.8 to +2.2.

VENUS is still a brilliant object, magnitude −3.9, in the morning skies before dawn but for observers in northern temperate latitudes it is only visible at a very low altitude above the eastern horizon for a short while. Indeed, for observers as far north as Scotland, Venus, even at sunrise, is always less than 5° above the eastern horizon.

MARS, magnitude +0.8, continues to be visible as an evening object in Leo, passing 1°N. of Regulus on May 24.

JUPITER, magnitude −2.5, is a conspicuous object in the southern skies, rising in the south-east in the early evening and still being visible in the south-west as morning twilight causes it to fade from view.

SATURN, magnitude +1.3, already in view to those further south, gradually becomes visible to observers in the British Isles during May, when they may detect it low above the east-south-east horizon before the morning twilight inhibits observation. Observers may be rather surprised to see the planet without its rings – the Earth actually passes through the ring plane on May 22.

FINLAY'S COMET. Another faint but well-known periodical comet, Finlay's, returns to perihelion on May 5. It was first seen by the South African astronomer W. H. Finlay on September 26, 1886, when it was of magnitude 8.5. The period was found to be about 7 years, and Finlay himself recovered it in 1893. Since then it has been seen at most returns, and its orbit is well known; once – in 1906 – it reached the fringe of naked-eye visibility, and in 1953 developed a short tail.

RUDOLPH MINKOWSKI. Rudolph Minkowski, the well-known German astronomer, was born a hundred years ago: on May 28, 1895. He came from Strasbourg, and took his degree at the University of Breslau, after which he worked at Hamburg Observatory for several years. In 1935 he emigrated to the United States, and remained there for the rest of his life.

He joined the staff of the Mount Wilson Observatory, and undertook a careful study of novæ and supernovæ, upon which he became one of the foremost authorities; he was also concerned with planetary nebulæ and stellar evolution. He was an active observer as well as a theorist, and made important contributions in many fields.

After the end of the war he became a pioneer in the science of radio astronomy, which was then, of course, comparatively new. His first concern was to identify radio sources with optical objects, and in this he was remarkably successful, finding both radio galaxies and supernova remnants. Working together with Walter Baade, he made great use of the Palomar 200-inch reflector, which at that period was not only the most powerful telescope in the world but was in a class of its own, and he made accurate measurements of the red shifts of many remote galaxies. After retiring from Mount Wilson, he became an active staff member of the Radio Astronomy Laboratory at Berkeley.

One of Minkowski's most important contributions concerned the nature of some particularly energetic radio sources. For example, Baade had believed Cygnus A to be due to galaxies in collision; Minkowski was able to show that this was not so. He supervised the National Geographic Society/Palomar Sky Survey, and received many honours, including the Bruce Medal of the Astronomical Society of the Pacific (1961). He died on January 4, 1976.

MERCURY AT DICHOTOMY. Mercury is at eastern elongation on May 22, and the theoretical phase is then 50 per cent (dichotomy). With Venus, the time of theoretical dichotomy does not usually agree with theory; during evening elongations dichotomy is early, while during morning elongations dichotomy is late. This so-called

'Schröter effect' is due to Venus's dense atmosphere. Mercury has no appreciable atmosphere, and therefore no comparable effect can be expected, but it is interesting to check the phase around the time of dichotomy – even though this is not easy with small telescopes. Daytime observation is to be recommended, provided that the observer is equipped with a telescope which has accurate setting circles.

Mercury has been bypassed by only one probe, Mariner 10, in the 1970s. It proved to have a crater-scarred surface not too unlike that of the moon, though with important differences in detail; unlike the moon, Mercury has a detectable magnetic field, and its heavy iron-rich core is probably larger than the whole lunar globe. More recently, Earth-based radar work has indicated the presence of ice inside some of the craters near the Mercurian poles, whose floors are always in shadow and which are therefore intensely cold. This is certainly unexpected; ice would not be anticipated on a world such as Mercury. Further investigations are needed before the presence of ice in these craters can be regarded as firmly established.

As yet we have mapped less than half the surface of Mercury; at each of the three active passes by Mariner 10 the same regions were in sunlight. Unfortunately, no more space-probes to Mercury have been funded as yet.

JUNE

New Moon: June 28

Full Moon: June 13

Solstice: June 21

MERCURY is at inferior conjunction on June 5, but then moves away from the Sun to reach greatest western elongation (22°) on June 29. The long summer twilight precludes observation from northern temperate latitudes. Visibility conditions improve as one travels south, and observers in the Southern Hemisphere will be able to locate the planet low above the east-north-east horizon about half-an-hour before sunrise, during the second half of the month.

VENUS continues to be visible as a brilliant object in the morning skies before dawn but is still situated so that observers in the Southern Hemisphere are favoured much more than those in the north. Its magnitude is −3.9. From the British Isles it can only be seen with difficulty for a few minutes before dawn, low above the east-north-east horizon. On June 19 Venus and Mercury are within 4° of each other.

MARS is no longer a conspicuous object, its magnitude being +1.1. It is still visible as an evening object in the western sky, in Leo.

JUPITER, magnitude −2.6, attains opposition on June 1 and therefore it is visible throughout the hours of darkness, observers in the British Isles seeing it move from south-east through south to south-west during the night. By the end of the month its retrograde motion has carried it back into Scorpius. Its path among the stars is shown in Figure 7. At opposition Jupiter is 647 million kilometres from the Earth.

SATURN is a morning object, in Aquarius, magnitude +1.2. It is visible in the south-eastern sky and for observers in the British Isles it will be visible low above the east-south-eastern horizon at mid-night, by the end of the month.

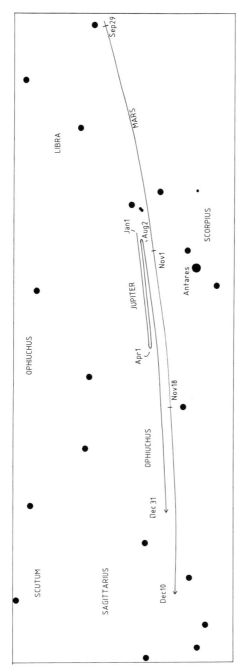

Figure 7. The paths of Mars and Jupiter.

THE GALILEANS. Jupiter comes to opposition this month, and though the altitude is rather inconveniently low for Northern Hemisphere observers there is a great deal of interest in following the movements and the phenomena of the four Galilean satellites. The Voyager results have shown us that the four are not alike. Ganymede and Callisto are icy and cratered; Europa icy and smooth; Io red and violently volcanic. It has been said that 'there is no such thing as an uninteresting Galilean'.

Ganymede is always the brightest of the four, and were it not so overpowered by the brilliant light of Jupiter it would be an easy naked-eye object. Callisto, nearly as large as Ganymede, is much less reflective, and is usually the faintest of the group. In colour Ganymede looks yellowish, Europa white, and Callisto often a curious hue which is not easy to define; some observers call it 'mauve'! Io does not appear so red telescopically as it might be expected to do from examination of the Voyager pictures, but in general it can be seen to have at least a perceptibly orange cast. The Hubble Space Telescope in its revised form is able to monitor the Ionian volcanoes, so that we will not have to wait for the arrival of a new mission – though Galileo, the space-probe named in honour of the great Italian, is due to reach the neighbourhood of Jupiter this year.

TWO CENTENARIES. The greatest of all seventeenth-century observers, Christiaan Huygens, was born in the Hague on April 14, 1629 and died there on June 8, 1695. His father was a famous Dutch statesman. Christiaan Huygens studied at Leyden, and became an expert observer; in 1655 he discovered Titan, the brightest satellite of Saturn, and was the first to explain the curious appearance of Saturn itself as being due to the presence of a flat ring. In 1659 he was the first to record a marking on the surface of Mars; his sketch shows the V-shaped feature known today as the Syrtis Major. In 1656 he was the first to give a detailed description of the Orion Nebula, though in fact he was not the first to record it (it had been seen by Nicholas Peiresc in 1610, and by Cysatus in 1618). In 1695 he made a sketch of the Nebula which clearly shows the four stars of the Trapezium, Theta Orionis.

Huygens was well aware that the stars are suns, and in many ways his views were in advance of their time. He made improvements to telescope design, inventing the 'Huyghenian' eyepiece, and he championed the wave theory of light; he is perhaps best remembered as the inventor of the pendulum clock. He settled in France in 1665, but religious persecution forced him to return to Holland, where he remained for the rest of his career.

Our other centenary is that of Daniel Kirkwood, who was born in Harford County, Maryland, on September 27, 1814 and became Professor of Mathematics at Delaware College; in 1856 he transferred to the University of Indiana. He was concerned mainly with comets and with meteors, which he declared were 'the débris of ancient, now disintegrated comets'; he explained the gaps in the asteroid zone, and these are still known as the Kirkwood Gaps. He died on June 11, 1895.

JULY

EARTH is at aphelion (furthest from the Sun) on July 4, at a distance of 152 million kilometres.

MERCURY is not suitably placed for observation by Northern Hemisphere observers, but for those near to and south of the Equator the planet will continue to be visible in the morning skies for the first half of the month, low above the east-north-east horizon before dawn. Thereafter Mercury will be too close to the Sun to be observable, as it reaches superior conjunction on July 28.

VENUS is drawing noticeably closer to the Sun, the interval of time available for observation before dawn by those in the Southern Hemisphere decreasing to zero before the end of the month. Observers in southern England will have great difficulty in seeing the planet, low above the east-north-east horizon, immediately before sunrise, even during the first half of the month.

MARS, magnitude +1.3, is still an evening object, low in the western sky. However, it is moving steadily south-eastwards, crossing the Equator towards the end of the month. This fact, coupled with the long duration of twilight, means that it will be lost to view by observers in the British Isles before the end of July.

JUPITER is a brilliant evening object in the southern skies, magnitude −2.4. By the end of the month observers in the British Isles will find it is no longer visible after midnight.

SATURN continues to be visible as a morning object in the south-eastern sky, magnitude +1.0.

URANUS is at opposition on July 21, in Sagittarius. The planet is only just visible to the naked eye under the best of conditions, since its magnitude is +5.6. In a small telescope it appears as a slightly greenish disk. At opposition Uranus is 2798 million kilometres from the Earth.

NEPTUNE is at opposition on July 17, at a distance of 4361 million kilometres. Neptune, like Uranus, is in Sagittarius. It is not visible to the naked eye, since its magnitude is +7.9.

URANUS AND NEPTUNE. The two outer giants still remain close together in the sky, though of course they are not true neighbours. One sometimes tends to forget the scale of the Solar System. On average, Uranus is 1783 million miles from the Sun, Neptune 2793 million miles; the difference is therefore well over a thousand million miles – much greater than the distance between the Sun and Saturn. And the distance between the orbits of Saturn and Uranus is much the same as that between the orbits of Saturn and the Earth!

The two planets are near twins in size; Uranus has an equatorial diameter of 31,770 miles, while that of Neptune is 31,410 miles (the values in kilometres are respectively 51,118 and 50,538). However, Neptune is appreciably the more massive, and unlike Uranus it has a strong internal heat-source. Uranus is a remarkably bland world, while Voyager showed Neptune to be dynamic; there are many surface features, notably the Great Dark Spot.

Both planets have obscure ring systems; both are radio sources, and both have magnetic fields with axes strongly inclined to the axes of rotation. The satellite systems are dissimilar. Titania, the largest of the Uranian family, has a diameter of 981 miles. Neptune's main satellite, Triton, is larger – 1681 miles in diameter – but all the indications are that Triton was once an independent body which was captured by Neptune; it may well be a planetesimal, and to be similar in nature to Pluto. Indeed, Triton is appreciably larger than Pluto.

Earth-based telescopes will show little or nothing on the pale disks of the outer giants, but they are always worth finding, and not for many years will they again be really close together in our sky.

D'ARREST'S COMET. Yet another famous periodical comet returns to perihelion this month (July 27). It was discovered on June 28, 1851 by Heinrich D'Arrest, the astronomer who was one of the co-discoverers of Neptune; he was working with Johann Galle with the Berlin telescope when the planet was found in 1846. The comet was of the tenth magnitude when first seen, and was found to have a period of between 6 and 7 years. It has been seen at most returns, and once, in 1976, it became as bright as magnitude 4.9, so that it was quite an easy naked-eye object; it developed a tail fully one degree long. The minimum distance from Earth was then no more than 14,000,000 miles, which by cometary standards is close. There are occasional close approaches to Jupiter; one occurred in 1990, and there will be others in 2034 and 2050.

D'Arrest himself was of French extraction, though he was born in Berlin and studied there; it was while at Berlin that he discovered his first comet, 1845 I, which reached the sixth magnitude but is classed as non-periodical (that is to say, it takes so long to complete its orbit round the Sun that we have no hope of recovering it). In 1857 he emigrated to Denmark, and lived in Copenhagen, where he carried out valuable work in stellar spectroscopy; he discovered three comets altogether, as well as one asteroid (Freia). He died in Copenhagen on June 14, 1875.

AUGUST

MERCURY is moving eastwards, away from the Sun: it is also moving southwards in declination so that it will not be suitably placed for observation in northern temperate latitudes. Opportunities for seeing Mercury improve as the observer's latitude decreases, and those in southern latitudes will be able to see the planet in the western evening sky, after the first ten days of the month. This evening apparition, which lasts until almost the end of September, is the most suitable one of the year for observers in southern latitudes. Figure 8 shows, for observers in latitude S.35°, the changes in azimuth (true bearing from the north through east, south, and west) and altitude of Mercury on successive evenings when the Sun is 6° below the horizon. This condition is known as the end of evening civil twilight and in this latitude and at this time of year occurs about 30 minutes after sunset. The changes in the brightness of the planet are indicated by the relative sizes of the circles marking Mercury's position at five-day intervals. It will be noticed that Mercury is at its brightest before it reaches greatest eastern elongation (27°) on September 9.

VENUS passes slowly through superior conjunction on August 20 and thus remains unsuitably placed for observation throughout the month.

MARS, magnitude +1.4, continues to be visible as an evening object in the western sky for observers in tropical and southern latitudes. Observers in the British Isles will not be able to see Mars again this year.

JUPITER, magnitude −2.2, continues to be visible as an evening object in the southern skies. After reaching its second stationary point on August 2 it resumes its direct motion.

SATURN, magnitude +0.9, is now visible for the greater part of the night as it approaches opposition next month. For the second time this year the Earth passes through the ring plane (on August 11), so that observers looking for the rings will be having a thin time of it!

LYRA. Lyra is a small constellation, but contains a remarkable number of interesting objects. Mythologically, it represents a harp given by Apollo to the great musician Orpheus. Though well north of the celestial equator, it is visible from almost all inhabited countries; only those who live in the southern part of New Zealand lose it.

The leading star, Vega, is of magnitude 0.0, and is surpassed only by Sirius, Canopus, Alpha Centauri, and Arcturus. It is 26 light-years away, so that it is one of our nearer neighbours, and is 52 times as luminous as the Sun; in 1983 IRAS, the Infra-Red Astronomical Satellite, detected cool material round it which may possibly be planet-forming, though it would certainly be premature to claim that an actual system of planets exists there. Vega is decidedly bluish in colour, and is a lovely sight in binoculars or a telescope.

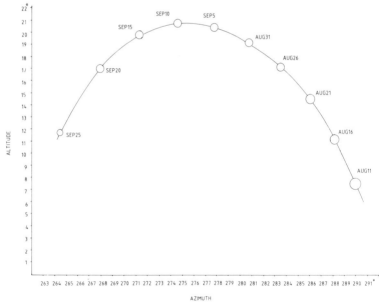

Figure 8. Evening apparition of Mercury for latitude S.35°.

Epsilon Lyræ, close to Vega in the sky, is a famous quadruple. Keen-sighted people can split the two main components without optical aid; the separation is almost 208 seconds of arc, and the components are not very unequal (magnitudes 4.7 and 5.1). A modest telescope will show that each component is again double. The real separation between the bright pairs is about two-tenths of a light-year; the distance from Earth is 180 light-years. All four components are hot and white.

Binoculars give a good view of another double, Delta Lyræ, where one component is red and the other white. With Zeta Lyræ the separation between the components is 44 seconds of arc, so that a small telescope will show them separately; the magnitudes are 4.3 and 5.9.

There are two bright variables in the constellation, Sheliak, or Beta Lyræ, is an eclipsing binary, and the prototype of its class. It differs from Algol in that the components are not very unequal, and are only about 22,000,000 miles apart, so that each must be drawn out into the shape of an egg. There are alternate deep and shallow minima; the maximum magnitude is 3.3, and the deeper minimum 4.3. The period is nearly 13 days. The adjacent Gamma Lyræ (magnitude 3.24) makes a useful comparison star.

The second bright variable is the red semi-regular R Lyræ; the range is from magnitude 4 to 5, and the period approximately 46 days. The nearest useful comparison star is Eta, magnitude 4.4.

Between Beta and Gamma lies the celebrated planetary nebula M.57 (see Figure 9), which is known as the Ring though recently it has been suggested that the true shape may be rather more

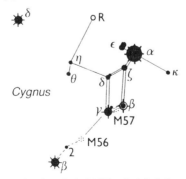

Figure 9. The nebula M.57 and global cluster M.56.

complex. A small telescope will show it, though a larger aperture is needed to bring out the dim central star. The nebula was first noted in 1779 by Darquier, who was using a telescope of only 3 inches aperture. The globular cluster M.56 was discovered by Messier in 1779; it lies not far from Albireo in Cygnus.

THE PERSEIDS. Do not forget to watch for the Perseid meteors. The shower is active for the whole of the first part of August, and can always be relied upon to produce a good display, though it is true that in 1995 moonlight will interfere; full Moon falls two days before the maximum of the shower on August 12.

The parent comet of the Perseids is Swift-Tuttle, discovered in 1862 when it was fairly bright. It was expected back in 1982, but failed to appear; it did finally come back in 1992, so that the period is 130 years rather than the anticipated 120. At the last return it was badly placed, but at the next perihelion passage it will come close to the Earth, and will be a magnificent object. It is a pity that nobody now alive will be able to see it!

SEPTEMBER

New Moon: September 24   *Full Moon:* September 9

Equinox: September 23

MERCURY continues to be visible in the evenings, though not for observers in northern temperate latitudes. For observers in the Southern Hemisphere it is a particularly favourable occasion since Mercury reaches aphelion on September 2, only seven days before greatest eastern elongation (27°). Reference should be made to Figure 8, given with the notes for August, where it will be seen that observers in the Southern Hemisphere will be able to see the planet for all except the last few days of the month.

VENUS is on the far side of its orbit relative to the Earth and although it is moving slowly away from the Sun it is unlikely to be seen as an evening object before next month.

MARS, for observers in equatorial and southern latitudes, is still visible as an evening object in the western sky. Its magnitude is +1.4, and by the end of the month it is only 40° from the Sun, no longer a conspicuous object.

JUPITER is still a brilliant object but by now has already crossed the meridian before sunset. It is still visible for several hours in the south-western sky. The magnitude of Jupiter is −2.1.

SATURN, magnitude +0.7, reaches opposition on September 14 and, as a result, is visible throughout the hours of darkness. At opposition its distance from the Earth is 1287 million kilometres. Saturn's path among the stars throughout the year is shown in Figure 10 (p. 104).

SATURN: EDGEWISE-ON. This year Saturn shows its customary beauty. The ring system is edgewise-on to us, and is by no means easy to see. It will be lost with small telescopes, and even large

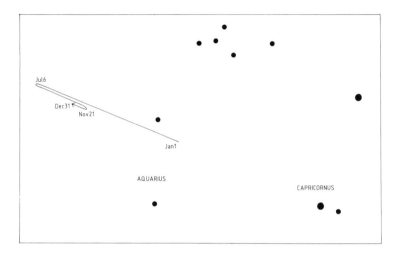

Figure 10. The path of Saturn in 1995.

apertures will be hard pressed to follow the ring system continuously. Yet there are interesting phenomena to be observed. For example, the two sides of the ring are sometimes unequal in brightness and in length, and occasional condensations have been reported in the very thin rings.

Moreover, the disk is well displayed – usually, part of it is covered – and this is a very good time to follow the satellites. Of the eighteen confirmed members of the Saturnian family, only the following are likely to be seen with telescopes of below 18 inches aperture:

Satellite	Mean distance from centre of Saturn (thousands of miles)	Diameter, miles (longest)	Magnitude
Mimas	115	261	12.9
Enceladus	148	318	11.8
Tethys	183	650	10.3
Dione	235	696	10.4
Rhea	328	950	9.7
Titan	760	3201	8.3
Hyperion	920	224	14.2
Iapetus	2200	892	9.6 to 12

Of the rest, there could be a chance of glimpsing Janus and Epimetheus, but both are less than 100,000 miles from Saturn; magnitudes 14.5 and 15.5 respectively. The remote asteroidal satellite Phœbe is of magnitude 16.5, and is a very difficult object indeed.

Obviously, satellite phenomena are hard to see except for Titan, and again apart from Titan all the satellites appear as nothing more than star-like points. Iapetus is of special interest, as it is very variable. When west of Saturn it can surpass Rhea; when east of the planet it becomes very dim – because its two hemispheres are of unequal albedo. The orbital period is 79 days.

Titan is one of the most interesting bodies in the entire Solar System. It is unique among planetary satellites in having an extensive atmosphere; indeed, the density is greater than that of the Earth's air, and the main constituent is nitrogen. It has been suggested that there may be life on Titan, but this seems unlikely to the highest degree. The surface temperature is about $-180°$ Centigrade, and the other main constituent of the atmosphere is methane. Whether the surface is solid, or whether part of it is covered with a methane or ethane ocean, is something which we hope to find out in the year 2004, with the landing there of a special space-craft, Huygens, carried to Saturn in the Cassini probe.

The escape velocity of Titan is 1.5 miles per second. This is much the same as that of our Moon – and yet the Moon is virtually airless. The reason why Titan can retain a dense atmosphere is that it is so cold; a low temperature reduces the speeds at which the atoms and molecules can move around, so that they find it less easy to escape.

Another suggestion is that when the Sun enters the red giant stage, as it must do in the far future, Titan will be warmed and perhaps become habitable. Alas for this idea! Even a small rise in temperature would lead to the abrupt departure of the atmosphere. When the Earth becomes intolerably hot, we cannot hope to save ourselves by mass migration to Titan!

Certainly it is worth paying attention to the satellites during the present opposition of Saturn. The rings will not again be edgewise-on until the year 2009.

FOMALHAUT. For northern observers, September evenings provide the best chances of locating Fomalhaut in the Southern Fish, the southernmost of the first-magnitude stars visible from Britain. Two of the stars in the Square of Pegasus (Scheat and Markab) point to it. From north Scotland, Fomalhaut barely rises; from Australia and New Zealand it is now not far from the zenith.

In 1983 IRAS, the Infra-Red Astronomical Satellite, found that Fomalhaut was one of the stars associated with cool, possibly planet-forming material which emitted in the infra-red (other similar 'infra-red excesses' were found with stars such as Vega and Beta Pictoris). Now, astronomers in Spain, using the radio telescope at Pico Veleta, claim that they have found Fomalhaut to be enveloped in a large, disk-like dust structure, extending out to 200 astronomical units from the star. This is not to say that Fomalhaut is attended by a system of planets, but at least such a thing is not impossible, and the leader of the 'Southern Fish' is a very interesting star indeed.

OCTOBER

New Moon: October 24   *Full Moon:* October 8

Summer Time in Great Britain and Northern Ireland ends on October 22.

MERCURY is at inferior conjunction on October 5, and then moves out from the Sun to its greatest western elongation (18°) on October 20. Thus it is a morning object, and for Northern Hemisphere observers this is the most suitable morning apparition of 1995. Figure 11 shows, for observers in latitude N.52°, the changes in azimuth (true bearing from the north through east, south, and west) and altitude of Mercury on successive mornings when the Sun is 6° below the horizon. This condition is known as the beginning of morning civil twilight and in this latitude and at this time of year occurs about 35 minutes before sunrise. The changes in the brightness of the planet are indicated by the relative sizes of the circles marking Mercury's position at five-day intervals. It will be noticed that Mercury is at its brightest after it reaches greatest western elongation (18°) on October 20.

VENUS, magnitude −3.9, is becoming visible in the evening sky, low in the west after sunset, though not yet available for observation by those in northern temperate latitudes.

MARS, magnitude +1.4, is still visible in the west-south-western sky in the early evenings, though not to those in latitudes north of the tropic of Cancer. Its path amongst the stars during the latter months of the year is shown in Figure 7, given with the notes for June.

JUPITER, magnitude −1.9, continues to be visible as a brilliant evening object, low in the south-western sky. Observers in the British Isles will find that by the end of the month it will only be visible for about an hour after sunset.

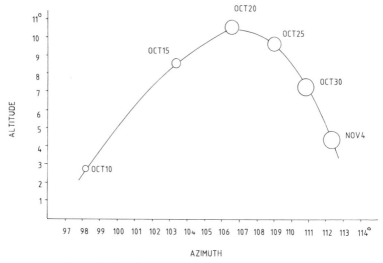

Figure 11. Morning apparition of Mercury for latitude N.52°.

SATURN is just past opposition and thus technically an evening object, though it is still visible through to the small hours of the morning, in the southern skies. Its magnitude is +0.8.

THE PENUMBRAL ECLIPSE OF THE MOON. As almost everyone knows, a lunar eclipse occurs when the Moon passes into the cone of shadow cast by the Earth. The average length of the Earth's shadow is 850,000 miles, so that at the mean distance of the Moon (239,000 miles) the diameter of the cone is about 5,700 miles, and is extensive enough to cover the Moon completely; totality may last for as long as 1 hour 44 minutes.

Because the Sun is a disk, and not a point source, there is a region of penumbra, or partial shadow, to either side of the main cone or umbra (see Figure 12). Obviously the Moon must pass through the penumbra before entering the umbra, but on some occasions the umbra is never reached, and the eclipse is penumbral only.

This is the case with the eclipse due on October 8. Penumbra will cover 83 per cent of the Moon; the greatest obscuration will be at 16ʰ 5ᵐ GMT. The dimming is slight, but should be perceptible with any telescope or even good binoculars, though whether it can be noticed with the naked eye is less certain – it depends mainly upon

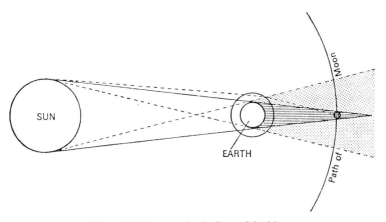

Figure 12. The penumbral eclipse of the Moon.

local conditions. It will be interesting to keep watch and see how great the penumbral dimming becomes.

The next true eclipses will be in 1996, on April 4 and September 27, both of which will be total and both of which should be well seen from Britain – clouds permitting!

SHEDIR AND SUSPECTED VARIABLES. The W of Cassiopeia is one of the most famous of far-northern constellations; during October evenings it is very high over Britain and the northern United States, though it is one of the groups inaccessible from most of Australia and South Africa, and all of New Zealand. The declination of Shedir, or Alpha Cassiopeiæ, is +57°.

Of the five stars of the W, one – Gamma, the middle member of the group – is variable; it is irregular, with a range of from magnitude 1.6 to 3.3, though for most of the time it hovers around 2.2. Shedir is a K-type orange star, and has been suspected of slight variability; the official magnitude is 2.3, but it may fluctuate between about 2.1 and 2.5. Beta Cassiopeiæ (2.27) makes a good comparison.

Shedir is one of a number of suspected naked-eye variables; another is Alphard or Alpha Hydræ, which was reported as variable by Sir John Herschel but whose fluctuations have never been confirmed. In G. F. Chambers' classic *Handbook of Astronomy*, published in 1890 in its fourth edition, there is a catalogue of suspected variables, a selection from which is given in Table 1.

TABLE 1

Star	Range	Authority and remarks
Gamma Pegasi	2½–3	Schwab; period 27½ days?
Nu Fornacis	5–6	Gould
z Eridani	4–6½	Houzeau, 1875
Gamma Eridani	2½–3½	Secchi
Pi¹ Orionis	3½–5	Gould; period 54½ days (Gage)
R Eridani	5½–6	Gould
Sigma Canis Majoris	4½–5	Gould; very red star
Beta Volantis	4–5	Gould
N Velorum	3½–4½	Gould; period 4½ days? Colour variable?
R Velorum	6½–7½	Thome
q Carinæ	4–5	Gould; red star
Eta Crateris	4½–6½	Houzeau, 1875
Epsilon Corvi	3–4	Gould
Gamma Corvi	2½–3	Gould
Delta Ursæ Majoris	2½–4	Pigott
Eta Virginis	3–4	Gould
Eta Ursæ Majoris	2–3	Espin
Upsilon Boötis	4–4½	Schmidt; reddish star
Theta Apodis	5½–6½	Gould; red star
Mu Draconis	4–5	S. J. Johnson
Iota Apodis	5–6	Gould
Beta Cygni	3–4	Klein; years?
Mu Aquilæ	4–5	Gould
Epsilon Draconis	3¾–4¾	Gould
Rho Pavonis	4½–5½	Gould
Upsilon Pavonos	5–6	Gould
Gamma Indi	6–6½	Gould
Beta Cephei	3–3½	Period 383 days?
Epsilon Pegasi	2–2½	Schwab; period 25¾ days?
Zeta Piscis Australis	5–6½	Schmidt, period long?
Eta Pegasi	3–3½	Christie
Iota Cephei	3½–4	Schmidt; period 369 days?
Iota Andromedæ	4½–5	Gore

Chambers' list of definite variables includes Beta Corvi (2½–3½; Smyth), which is in fact constant at magnitude 2.65. The other cases he lists are unconfirmed and probably spurious; all the same, naked-eye observers may care to watch a few of them!

NOVEMBER

New Moon: November 22   *Full Moon:* November 7

MERCURY is still visible as a morning object, magnitude −0.9, low above the east-south-east horizon for a short while before dawn, but only for the first few days of the month. Thereafter it is unsuitably placed for observation as it passes slowly through superior conjunction on November 23.

VENUS, already available for observation by observers further south, gradually becomes visible as a brilliant evening object, magnitude −3.9, low in the south-western sky after sunset, for observers in northern temperate latitudes.

MARS, magnitude +1.3, is moving towards the Sun and even for those in southern latitudes it will be lost to view over the west-south-western horizon soon after sunset. Observers with telescopes might be able to detect Mars on the evening of November 22 as Venus passes only 11 arcminutes south of Mars at 22ʰ GMT.

JUPITER is coming towards the end of its period of visibility this month and is only visible low in the south-western sky for a short while after sunset. Its magnitude is −1.8. By the end of the month it is only 15° from the Sun, which means that for observers in the British Isles it is only about 5° above the horizon at sunset. Observers should note that Venus is near Jupiter for a few days around November 19 when Mars is also close by.

SATURN, magnitude +0.9, continues to be visible as an evening object in the southern skies.

BERTIL LINDBLAD. November 26 is the centenary of the birth of Bertil Lindblad, one of Sweden's greatest astronomers. He was born at Örebo, graduated at Uppsala, and in 1927 became Director of the Stockholm Observatory following a spell at Mount Wilson. In 1931 he organized the removal of the main equipment to the far better site of Saltsjöbaden, and fully modernized it.

Lindblad was a pioneer in the studies of rotations of galaxies, and was the first to show that with spirals the arms are 'trailing'. He also made major contributions to studies of stellar evolution and galactic structure. He served as President of the International Astronomical Union from 1948 to 1952, and was awarded the Gold Medals of the Royal Astronomical Society and of the Astronomical Society of the Pacific. He died on June 25, 1965.

THE LEONID METEORS. The Leonids are the most unpredictable of all annual meteor showers. Generally they are sparse, but throughout the last thousand years or so they have provided occasional 'storms' – as in 1799, 1833, 1866, and 1966. The average interval between storms is 33 years, though those of 1899 and 1933 did not occur because of planetary perturbations.

The parent comet is Tempel–Tuttle, which has a long history. It was discovered in December 1865 by W. Tempel, and independently in the following month by Horace Tuttle; it reached magnitude 5.5, and produced a definite tail. The period was given as 33 years, and the comet was identified with those of 1366 – which reached the third magnitude – and 1699. It was recovered in 1965, and is due back at perihelion in 1999.

Leonid 'storms' occur when the comet is near perihelion, and there is a very good chance that one will be seen in 1999; but it is possible that activity will start to build up well before that, and meteor observers will certainly be very much on the alert from now on. The maxima of the storms are brief – that of 1966 occurred during daylight in Europe, and little was seen during the period of darkness. We cannot be sure that the Leonids will again produce spectacular displays, but the omens are encouraging even if not much can really be expected before November 1998.

A CURIOUS ANOMALY. The southernmost of the first-magnitude stars is Achernar, or Alpha Eridani – the 'Last in the River'. With its declination of $-57°$ it is inaccessible from any part of Europe or the United States; during November evenings it is near the zenith from Australia and New Zealand. It is of magnitude 0.46, so that it is the ninth brightest star in the whole of the sky; it is 85 light-years away, and 750 times as luminous as the Sun. The spectral type is B5, so that it is a white or bluish-white star with a high surface temperature.

Yet in Chambers' list of red stars, published in 1890, it is given as 'red'! Chambers is usually very reliable, but this is not a misprint in the fourth edition of his book, as it is repeated elsewhere.

The conclusion must be that he had never seen it for himself, and had taken a faulty estimate from some other source. Certainly there is not the slightest chance that Achernar has changed colour, and this serves to show that it is not always wise to take colour records at face value. Remember that in some old works Sirius too is given as a red star . . .

Achernar is easy to find, partly because it is so bright and partly because there are no other brilliant stars close to it. The south pole of the sky, not marked by any bright star, lies about midway between Achernar and the Southern Cross – so that when Achernar is high up the Cross is low down, and vice versa.

OCTANS. The south polar constellation is very dim; the brightest star, Nu, is only of magnitude 3.8. The south polar star is Sigma, magnitude 5.5. It is less than one degree from the pole at the present time; the distance from the pole was only 45' in 1900, but is now increasing, and will have reached a full degree by the end of the century. It is a star of spectral type FO, about 7 times as luminous as the Sun and 120 light-years away. Certainly it is a very poor substitute for the northern Polaris!

DECEMBER

New Moon: December 22   *Full Moon:* December 7

Solstice: December 22

MERCURY becomes visible to observers in equatorial and southern latitudes after the first fortnight in December, low above the south-western horizon, about half-an-hour after sunset. Observers in northern temperate latitudes will have to wait until early in the New Year before having an opportunity to see the planet.

VENUS is a brilliant evening object, magnitude −3.9. It gradually becomes visible for longer and longer after sunset as the month progresses. Observers in northern temperate latitudes will still only be viewing the planet at a very low altitude above the south-western horizon.

MARS is unsuitably placed for observation.

JUPITER is in conjunction with the Sun on December 18 and is therefore unsuitably placed for observation throughout the month. The only exception to this statement is that it might just be detected by keen-sighted observers in the Southern Hemisphere, observing with a good south-western horizon at the end of evening civil twilight, for the first few days of the month.

SATURN, magnitude +1.1, is still visible as an evening object in the south-western sky.

COLUMBA AND CÆLUM. Two small southern constellations are on view during December evenings in the general area of Orion and Canis Major. Columba, the Dove, was introduced to the sky in 1679 by an otherwise obscure astronomer named Royer, who was also the first to introduce the Southern Cross as a separate constellation (previously the Cross had been included in Centaurus, which practically surrounds it). Columba seems to represent the dove which Noah released from the Ark, and was originally Columba Noachi, Noah's Dove.

It is not at all prominent, and from the latitude of Britain it is always very low; in fact the star Eta Columbæ (magnitude 3.96) never rises at all from anywhere in the British Isles. The brightest stars are Alpha or Phakt (magnitude 2.64) and Beta or Wazn (3.12). There is nothing of interest in Columba to the user of a small telescope.

Adjoining it is Cælum, the Graving Tool – originally Cælum Sculptoris. It was created by Lacaille in 1752, but for no good reason, because it has no star above the fourth magnitude and only two above the fifth; it is devoid of interesting objects, and seems to have no justification for separate identity. It is so far south that from Britain it is more or less inaccessible.

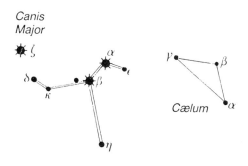

Figure 13.

Cælum is one of a number of small, dim, 'modern' constellations. One tends to sympathize with the great last-century astronomer Sir John Herschel, who commented that the constellation patterns seemed to have been devised so as to cause as much confusion and inconvenience as possible!

Two CENTENARIES. The Danish astronomer Peter Andreas Hansen was born two hundred years ago, on December 8, 1795, at Tondern. He taught himself mathematics and astronomy, and became assistant at Altona Observatory in 1821 before transferring to Seeberg, near Gotha, four years later. His researches were purely mathematical; he became the chief contemporary authority on the subject of the movements of the Moon. He died at Gotha on March 28, 1874.

John Russell Hind was born at Nottingham on May 12, 1823. Between 1840 and 1843 he was assistant at Greenwich, and then became director of George Bishop's private observatory in Regent's Park, Central London (of which nothing now remains, and in any case the present-day light pollution makes Regent's Park quite useless as an observing site). He discovered a number of asteroids: Iris and Flora (1847), Irene (1851), Melpomene and Fortuna (1852), Euterpe (1853) and Urania (1854) as well as Nova Ophiuchi (1848), which rose to the fourth magnitude. It is clear that he was an expert observer; in 1853 he also became Superintendent of the Nautical Almanac. Much of his work was carried out with the 7-inch refractor at Regent's Park.

Hind was also one of the first to confirm the discovery of Neptune in 1846. He received notification of the discovery from Brünnow, in Germany, and made haste to search for the new world; on September 30, 1846 he identified it without difficulty, and wrote a letter about it to the London *Times*. It was this letter which made James Challis, vainly searching for the planet at Cambridge, realize that he had been forestalled. Hind died on December 23, 1895.

THE LAST APOLLO. It is worth recalling that it is now well over twenty years since the end of the Apollo programme; it was in December 1972 that Eugene Cernan and Harrison Schmitt, from Apollo 17, landed on the Moon, while their colleague, the late Ronald Evans, remained in orbit. That mission marked the end of the first phase of lunar exploration by rocket; the next American lunar probe was delayed until Clementine was launched in 1994.

Eclipses in 1995

During 1995 there will be three eclipses, two of the Sun and one of the Moon.

1. *A partial eclipse of the Moon on April 15* is visible from the western part of North and Central America, the Pacific Ocean, Antarctica, Australasia, the Indian Ocean, and eastern and central Asia. The eclipse begins at 11^h 41^m and ends at 12^h 55^m. At maximum eclipse 12 per cent of the Moon is obscured (a small portion of the north limb).

2. *An annular eclipse of the Sun on April 29* is visible as a partial eclipse from the eastern part of the central and southern Pacific, Central and South America, southern Mexico, Florida and the West Indies, the Atlantic Ocean, and the extreme west of North Africa. The eclipse begins at 14^h 33^m and ends at 20^h 32^m. The track of the annular phase crosses South America from the Peru–Ecuador border through northern Brazil. The annular phase begins at 15^h 40^m and ends at 19^h 25^m: the maximum duration is 6^m 37^s.

3. *A total eclipse of the Sun on October 24* is visible as a partial eclipse from extreme East Africa, Arabia, most of Asia (except the north-east), part of the Indian Ocean, Australasia except southern Australia and New Zealand, and the western Pacific Ocean. The eclipse begins at 1^h 52^m and ends at 7^h 13^m. The path of totality starts in Iran, crosses Afghanistan, Pakistan, India, Burma, Thailand, Cambodia, South Vietnam, and North Borneo, and ends in the western Pacific Ocean. The total phase begins at 2^h 52^m and ends at 6^h 13^m: the maximum duration is 2^m 10^s.

Occultations in 1995

In the course of its journey round the sky each month, the Moon passes in front of all the stars in its path, and the timing of these occultations is useful in fixing the position and motion of the Moon. The Moon's orbit is tilted at more than five degrees to the ecliptic, but it is not fixed in space. It twists steadily westwards at a rate of about twenty degrees a year, a complete revolution taking 18.6 years, during which time all the stars that lie within about six and a half degrees of the ecliptic will be occulted. The occultations of any one star continue month after month until the Moon's path has twisted away from the star, but only a few of these occultations will be visible at any one place in hours of darkness.

There are four occultations of bright planets in 1995, one of Mercury, two of Venus and one of Mars.

Only four first-magnitude stars are near enough to the ecliptic to be occulted by the Moon: these are Regulus, Aldebaran, Spica, and Antares. Only Spica undergoes an occultation (six times) in 1995.

Predictions of these occultations are made on a world-wide basis for all stars down to magnitude 7.5, and sometimes even fainter. The British Astronomical Association has just produced the first complete lunar occultation prediction package for microcomputer users.

Recently occultations of stars by planets (including minor planets) and satellites have aroused considerable attention.

The exact timing of such events gives valuable information about positions, sizes, orbits, atmospheres and sometimes of the presence of satellites. The discovery of the rings of Uranus in 1977 was the unexpected result of the observations made of a predicted occultation of a faint star by Uranus. The duration of an occultation by a satellite or minor planet is quite small (usually of the order of a minute or less). If observations are made from a number of stations it is possible to deduce the size of the planet.

The observations need to be made either photoelectrically or visually. The high accuracy of the method can readily be appreciated when one realizes that even a stop-watch timing accurate to $0^s.1$ is, on average, equivalent to an accuracy of about 1 kilometre in the chord measured across the minor planet.

Comets in 1995

The appearance of a bright comet is a rare event which can never be predicted in advance, because this class of object travels round the Sun in an enormous orbit with a period which may well be many thousands of years. There are therefore no records of the previous appearances of these bodies, and we are unable to follow their wanderings through space.

Comets of short period, on the other hand, return at regular intervals, and attract a good deal of attention from astronomers. Unfortunately they are all faint objects, and are recovered and followed by photographic methods using large telescopes. Most of these short-period comets travel in orbits of small inclination which reach out to the orbit of Jupiter, and it is this planet which is mainly responsible for the severe perturbations which many of these comets undergo. Unlike the planets, comets may be seen in any part of the sky, but since their distances from the Earth are similar to those of the planets their apparent movements in the sky are also somewhat similar, and some of them may be followed for long periods of time.

The following periodic comets are expected to return to perihelion in 1994, and to be brighter than magnitude +15.

Comet	Year of discovery	Period (years)	Predicted date of perihelion 1995
de Vico-Swift	1884	7.3	Apr. 9
Finlay	1886	6.8	May 5
Clark	1973	5.5	May 31
D'Arrest	1851	6.5	July 27
Tuttle-Giacobini-Kresak	1858	5.5	July 28
Reinmuth (1)	1928	7.3	Sept. 3
Schwassmann-Wachmann (3)	1930	5.3	Sept. 22
Jackson-Neujmin	1936	8.2	Oct. 6
Longmore	1975	7.0	Oct. 9
Perrine-Mrkos	1896	6.8	Dec. 6
Honda-Mrkos-Pajdusakova	1948	5.3	Dec. 25

Minor Planets in 1995

Although many thousands of minor planets (asteroids) are known to exist, only 3,000 of these have well-determined orbits and are listed in the catalogues. Most of these orbits lie entirely between the orbits of Mars and Jupiter. All of these bodies are quite small, and even the largest, Ceres, is only about 960 kilometres in diameter. Thus, they are necessarily faint objects, and although a number of them are within the reach of a small telescope few of them ever reach any considerable brightness. The first four that were discovered are named Ceres, Pallas, Juno and Vesta. Actually the largest four minor planets are Ceres, Pallas, Vesta and Hygeia (excluding 2060 Chiron, which orbits mainly between the paths of Saturn and Uranus, and whose nature is uncertain). Vesta can occasionally be seen with the naked eye and this is most likely to occur when an opposition occurs near June, since Vesta would then be at perihelion. Approximate dates of opposition (and magnitude) for these minor planets in 1995 are:

1 Ceres

1995		2000.0 Right Ascension		Declination		*Geocentric distance*	*Visual mag.*	*Elongation*
month	*day*	*hr.*	*min.*	°	′			°
1	1	9	44.25	+25	23.2	1.750	7.5	139.1W
1	11	9	40.60	+26	43.0	1.676	7.2	149.5W
1	21	9	34.24	+28	7.1	1.624	7.0	159.4W
1	31	9	25.82	+29	26.8	1.599	6.9	165.9W
2	10	9	16.42	+30	33.0	1.602	6.9	163.6E
2	20	9	7.36	+31	18.9	1.632	7.1	154.9E
3	2	8	59.88	+31	41.8	1.686	7.3	144.7E
3	12	8	54.91	+31	42.3	1.762	7.5	134.6E
3	22	8	52.91	+31	23.7	1.854	7.7	124.9E
4	1	8	53.94	+30	49.3	1.960	7.9	115.7E

2 Pallas

1995		Right Ascension		Declination		Geocentric distance	Visual mag.	Elongation
		2000.0						
month	day	hr.	min.	°	′			°
1	1	3	15.67	−28	13.0	1.817	8.4	108.2E
1	11	3	16.64	−26	26.9	1.880	8.5	102.3E
1	21	3	20.51	−24	21.8	1.947	8.6	96.6E
1	31	3	27.07	−22	4.1	2.017	8.7	91.1E
2	10	3	36.07	−19	38.9	2.087	8.7	85.9E
2	20	3	47.21	−17	10.5	2.158	8.8	80.9E
3	2	4	.23	−14	42.1	2.228	8.8	76.2E
3	12	4	14.91	−12	16.9	2.296	8.9	71.7E
3	22	4	31.03	− 9	57.1	2.364	8.9	67.3E
4	1	4	48.40	− 7	44.8	2.431	8.9	63.1E

3 Juno

1995		Right Ascension		Declination		Geocentric distance	Visual mag.	Elongation
		2000.0						
month	day	hr.	min.	°	′			°
6	1	18	2.94	− 5	7.1	2.308	10.2	152.7W
6	11	17	55.01	− 4	49.5	2.260	10.0	159.4W
6	21	17	46.39	− 4	44.2	2.238	10.0	161.1E
7	1	17	37.82	− 4	52.1	2.244	10.0	156.6E
7	11	17	30.06	− 5	12.7	2.276	10.1	148.6E

4 Vesta

1995		Right Ascension		Declination		Geocentric distance	Visual mag.	Elongation
		2000.0						
month	day	hr.	min.	°	′			°
1	1	6	5.50	+21	33.7	1.582	6.5	170.9E
1	11	5	55.11	+22	3.1	1.613	6.7	158.5E
1	21	5	46.78	+22	30.5	1.671	6.9	146.4E
1	31	5	41.30	+22	56.1	1.751	7.1	135.0E
2	10	5	39.05	+23	20.3	1.849	7.3	124.4E
2	20	5	40.05	+23	43.5	1.960	7.5	114.5E
3	2	5	44.04	+24	5.2	2.080	7.7	105.4E
3	12	5	50.74	+24	24.8	2.204	7.8	96.9E
3	22	5	59.75	+24	41.4	2.330	7.9	89.0E
4	1	6	10.75	+24	53.9	2.455	8.0	81.6E

A vigorous campaign for observing the occultations of stars by the minor planets has produced improved values for the dimensions of some of them, as well as the suggestion that some of these planets may be accompanied by satellites. Many of these observations have been made photoelectrically. However, amateur observers have found renewed interest in the minor planets since it has been shown that their visual timings of an occultation of a star by a minor planet are accurate enough to lead to reliable determinations of diameter. As a consequence many groups of observers all over the world are now organizing themselves for expeditions should the predicted track of such an occultation cross their country.

In 1984 the British Astronomical Association formed a special Asteroid and Remote Planets Section.

Meteors in 1995

Meteors ('shooting stars') may be seen on any clear moonless night, but on certain nights of the year their number increases noticeably. This occurs when the Earth chances to intersect a concentration of meteoric dust moving in an orbit around the Sun. If the dust is well spread out in space, the resulting shower of meteors may last for several days. The word 'shower' must not be misinterpreted – only on very rare occasions have the meteors been so numerous as to resemble snowflakes falling.

If the meteor tracks are marked on a star map and traced backwards, a number of them will be found to intersect in a point (or a small area of the sky) which marks the radiant of the shower. This gives the direction from which the meteors have come.

The following table gives some of the more easily observed showers with their radiants; interference by moonlight is shown by the letter M.

Limiting dates	Shower	Maximum	R.A. h	R.A. m	Dec. °	
Jan. 1–4	Quadrantids	Jan. 4	15	28	+50	
April 20–22	Lyrids	Apr. 21	18	08	+32	M
May 1–8	Aquarids	May 5	22	20	0	
June 17–26	Ophiuchids	June 20	17	20	−20	M
July 15–Aug. 15	Delta Aquarids	July 29	22	36	−17	
July 15–Aug. 20	Piscis Australids	July 31	22	40	−30	
July 15–Aug. 25	Capricornids	Aug. 2	20	36	−10	
July 27–Aug. 17	Perseids	Aug. 12	3	04	+58	M
Oct. 15–25	Orionids	Oct. 22	6	24	+15	
Oct. 26–Nov. 16	Taurids	Nov. 3	3	44	+14	M
Nov. 15–19	Leonids	Nov. 17	10	08	+22	M
Dec. 9–14	Geminids	Dec. 13	7	28	+32	M
Dec. 17–24	Ursids	Dec. 23	14	28	+78	

M = moonlight interferes

Some Events in 1996

ECLIPSES

There will be four eclipses, two of the Sun and two of the Moon.

April 3–4: total eclipse of the Moon – western Asia, Europe, Americas.

April 17: partial eclipse of the Sun – New Zealand.

September 27: total eclipse of the Moon – western Asia, Europe, Americas.

October 12: partial eclipse of the Sun – Canada, Europe, N. Africa.

THE PLANETS

Mercury may be seen more easily from northern latitudes in the evenings about the time of greatest eastern elongation (April 23) and in the mornings around greatest western elongation (October 3). In the Northern Hemisphere the corresponding dates are February 11 (morning) and August 21 (evening).

Venus is visible in the evenings until May and in the mornings from mid-June to December.

Mars is visible in the mornings from June to December.

Jupiter is at opposition on July 4.

Saturn is at opposition on September 26.

Uranus is at opposition on July 25.

Neptune is at opposition on July 18.

Pluto is at opposition on May 22.

Explosion!

DAVID ALLEN

There's an old jingle, that for want of better knowledge, I shall attribute to the ubiquitous Anon. Because of its age, it is couched in sexist language, but I know of no rhyme that will correct this peccadillo. It runs:

> *The difference between men and boys*
> *is that men have more expensive toys.*

Professional observing often reminds me of this jingle. As a boy I explored the beauties of the night sky with a small telescope, only a couple of inches aperture. But as my years accumulated I came to use progressively larger instruments, telescopes designed not for sightseeing, but for serious research. Yet the thrill of observing, now so sophisticated, remains as great as ever. Is it work . . . or is it play? For me the answer is play. Those few nights per year when I am at the controls are my reward for the tedium that characterizes a large portion of a research life, much to the surprise of those who have never been exposed to it. Yes, for me a telescope is a magnificent toy.

Though all nights are thrilling, just occasionally comes one that stands apart. These are the nights when a particularly difficult observation was pulled off, or even better, a night on which I made a discovery, and knew it.

Discovery is a rare thing in astronomy. For 99 per cent of the time – more perhaps – the observations one plans and undertakes are merely seeking to answer a question one has formulated, adding one more piece to the jigsaw research one is attempting. Discovery, true discovery, is not planned, it is serendipitous. Discoveries are usually made because researchers have misjudged the way the Universe is put together, have gone looking for one piece of evidence and found, instead, another. Such discoveries are memorable. But for sheer thrill you can't beat the truly unexpected, serendipitous discovery. One such happened in September 1992.

The particular toy I was playing with was the infrared camera

IRIS recently built for use on the Anglo-Australian Telescope in New South Wales, Australia. Some of the fascinating results this camera has given us were featured in the *1993 Yearbook*. They fascinate because the eye does not respond to infrared wavelengths, and many celestial objects take on quite different guises.

In September 1992 IRIS was still young as instruments go, and although observations had been underway for eighteen months there were still features of it that needed testing. One of these was a new filter we had just installed. Filters select the particular wavelength or colour of infrared radiation the instrument responds to, and observations through different filters allow one to deduce more about an object. The particular filter I was testing selected a single emission line of iron, so that an object would show through it only if conditions were just right for the iron to glow. In practice, that meant that the iron must be within a gas cloud that was moving through another at a speed of a few hundred kilometres per second. This sort of speed is often found in the outflowing gas from exploding stars and supernovæ, and we had bought the filter primarily to study the remnants of prehistoric supernovæ.

My tests ended a little before dawn began to pale the sky. The filter appeared to perform as expected. I decided to use the remaining time to make a picture of the Orion Nebula. This famous feature must be one of the most widely observed objects in the sky. Little did I dream that there could be anything left to discover in it.

I made observations through three filters so that they could be played back on to the red, green, and blue channels of a colour video. Often it is the juxtaposition of two or three filters in this way that reveals features one might never pick out singly. Because the Orion Nebula is big, I set the telescope to map it by taking a series of twenty-five small pictures through each filter, in a five by five grid. I could then sit back and watch the pictures one by one as they appeared on the camera's screen.

I chose first a filter that picks out hydrogen molecules. Most of the constellation of Orion is an ocean of hydrogen molecules, but the filter identifies disturbed places, again where one gas cloud is jostling another. I watched the familiar patterns of the Nebula as each of its twenty-five-piece jigsaw flashed into view and was in turn replaced by the next. The telescope made its way towards the north-west quadrant, where I knew that five long finger-like projections of glowing hydrogen molecules lay. These puzzling features had been found some years earlier, by my colleagues Ken Taylor and John Storey, using a much simpler infrared instrument also on the Anglo-Australian Telescope.

Conditions were very good, and in particular the atmosphere was extremely steady. With IRIS I anticipated seeing the fingers in greater detail, but I was not prepared for what appeared on the display screen. It was the ninth of the twenty-five positions that picked them up, and as it was displayed I saw that each finger was resolved into a series of hollow features looking for all the world like the wakes behind a succession of speed boats. There were far more than five of these wakes, though many of them overlapped so that in less good conditions they would have led one to see just the five fingers we thought we knew of.

I had but a minute or so to consider the scene before the next jigsaw piece appeared on the screen, obliterating the wakes till I had a chance to examine the data afresh, potentially several days later.

I switched to the iron filter and repeated the jigsaw. Not much of interest appeared till we reached the same ninth segment. Suddenly the screen flashed up a host of diffuse, bright blobs. I sat up straight and stared at the patterns. It seemed to my tired, end-of-night brain that the positions of the iron blobs corresponded to where I had half an hour earlier seen the tips of the hydrogen wakes.

So strong was this impression that, when dawn finally came and it was time to pack up, I didn't head off for bed as I should have done, but spent an hour or so working up the data to have a better look. There were about twenty hydrogen wakes, and, sure enough, the iron blobs *did* align with them, their heads exactly where the speed boats would have been.

The interpretation was obvious. At least a score of blobs had been hurled out into the Orion Nebula. Each was travelling so fast that at its head hydrogen molecules were broken apart into atoms, and thus didn't glow in the hydrogen filter I used first. But iron was made to glow strongly. Behind each a wake ran, like the shock wave from a supersonic aircraft. And just as it hurts less to be hit by the shock wave than by the aircraft itself, so in these wakes in the Orion Nebula the shock wasn't violent enough either to smash apart hydrogen molecules or to drive the iron to glow. But it did make the hydrogen molecules glow. Fortuitously, by using these two filters, I had picked out the very information needed to interpret the discovery.

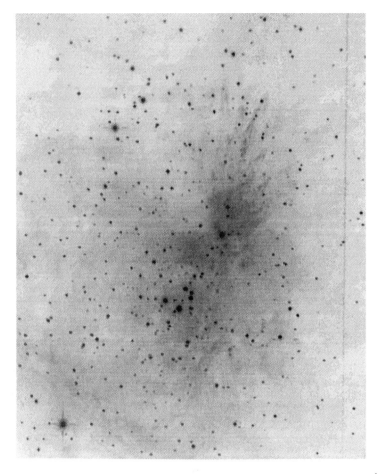

Figure 1. The Orion Nebula in the infrared. This and subsequent pictures are presented in the negative, with black stars on a white sky, to show better the filaments of nebulosity. The Trapezium stars are below and to the left of centre: they excite the nebula to glow and are very prominent in a small telescope. Above and right of centre is the second group of stars, much younger and seen only at infrared wavelengths, that includes IRc2. The wakes of glowing hydrogen molecules emanate from this region, appearing above them on this picture.

I sought the help of my friend Michael Burton, an expert on the effects of shock waves in gas. Together we studied the pictures. We also obtained a few new observations that told us how fast the iron blobs were moving, and found a speed of about 400 kilometres *per second*.

Back in my office I carefully plotted the centre lines of each wake. They radiated outwards from a point in the Orion Nebula. Clearly something almost explosive had occurred here, ejecting gassy blobs of shrapnel at very high speed. The centre of the explosion was right where the youngest stars are still being made. Indeed, it looked to coincide with the youngest star we know in the nebula, a star with the boring catalogue name of IRc2. From the speed and the distance they had travelled we could determine how long ago this explosion occurred. The answer was 1000 years. Others who had studied the star IRc2 had suggested that it's only about 1000 years old. The implication is clear.

This is astonishingly young. Stars like the Sun live for thousands of millions of years. Even really big stars, as we believe IRc2 to be, see out many millions of years. They are also pretty rare: we can catalogue only a few hundred in our Galaxy. To encounter one so young is as unlikely as sampling the houses in your street and finding a child a few days old. We are, in fact, very lucky to have so young a star as close to us as the Orion Nebula, which lies about 1600 light-years away: we chose the right street to live on.

Michael and I made an estimate of the amount of gas in each bit of shrapnel. They turned out to be as massive as a planet, though much more diffuse. When ejected they would have been quite compact, expanding as they travelled outwards. Now, to make something as massive as a planet travel at 400 km/sec requires a devil of a lot of energy, and we could estimate that the energy imparted by the explosion is at least as much as the total energy output by the Sun in the intervening millenium. Since it looks as though the bits of shrapnel were all blown out in a relatively short time, we are dealing with something much more energetic than our Sun.

We could think of two possible reasons for an explosion. One is the phenomenon of a supernova. Massive stars, such as those forming in the Orion Nebula, end their lives in dramatic supernova explosions that completely disrupt the star. Supernovæ are, however, much more energetic even than the explosion I had found, and it would be hard to hide the extra energy. So we preferred to explain the event as a *fuor*.

What, you will be asking, is a *fuor*? These rare phenomena get their name from the first one ever seen, a star in the constellation

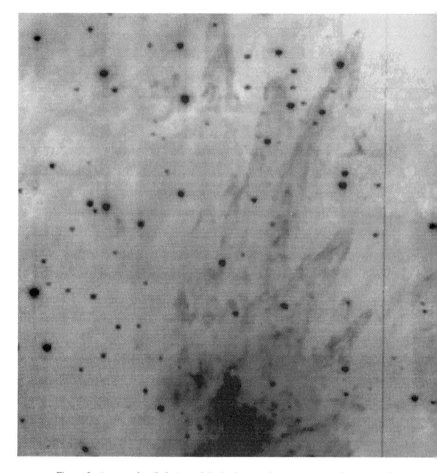

Figure 2. A more detailed view of the hydrogen shows many overlapping wakes.

Orion that bore the catalogue designation FU Orionis. This star rose to prominence when it suddenly and dramatically brightened by a factor of about 1000. Before the brightening little was known of it; subsequently it has settled down almost to resemble a normal star, but at the new, bright level. We know it to be very young, and we think this may be a common phase in the evolution of very young stars. There are some heady technical theories about what causes

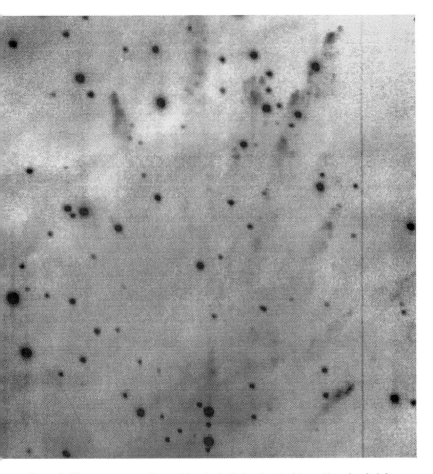

Figure 3. The same area as Figure 2 but in the light of excited iron. Note the slightly fuzzy blobs in addition to the stars. Most of the blobs lie exactly at the heads of hydrogen wakes. The two brightest blobs have no wakes. They have presumably been ejected somewhat towards us and have broken out of the densest parts of the nebula so that there is insufficient hydrogen to make visible wakes, while they themselves become more visible.

the brightening that I don't have space to describe here. Suffice to say that the handful of fuors now known are all small stars – Sun sized. We have never seen a fuor event take place in a much bigger star, a star like IRc2 for instance. It's a guess, in truth, that IRc2 underwent a fuor outburst, though it seems eminently reasonable that if it did it would be a much more dramatic and energetic example than we have witnessed in the Sun-sized stars.

It's another guess that a fuor can project blobs of gas around at wildly supersonic speeds, though there are reasonable grounds for that belief.

Once we had published the discovery, in the journal *Nature*, it began to attract a great deal of attention. Nothing like it has been seen before. We have encountered young stars that spray out a steady jet of gas, but that's a much less energetic activity involving relatively tiny amounts of the gas. They do it steadily, not explosively, and they produce only one (or perhaps two exactly opposite) jets. The IRc2 phenomenon is a new twist on the old story of young stars finding themselves with excess gas they have to get rid of before they can settle down to normal lives. A cottage industry is developing as people rush to examine how the explosion relates to the gas recorded by radio astronomers; to develop theories for the exact explosion mechanism; to test the understanding of how shocks percolate through gas; to study the blobs at other wavelengths; or simply to seek new observations of IRc2 itself that might shed some light on its past. And, of course, there are searches for other examples elsewhere in the sky, to gain clues from specimens of different ages, and to determine how widespread the phenomenon is.

In this last case we have to ask what a similar event would have looked like 1000 years ago, or 1000 years hence, for though it is inconceivable that this is the only case in the observable part of the Universe, it is equally unlikely that the next we find will also be 1000 years old. Would we recognize an event like this 2000, 5000, 10,000 years old? Quite possibly not with our present understanding.

From my perspective the best part of this saga has already passed – the discovery. But there remains a fascination to watch this cottage industry blossom, and to be involved in one or two of the threads of research I have just listed. It will be a good few years before we have a comprehensive suite of answers, and I shall enjoy each as it arrives.

A Star is Disassembled

PAUL MURDIN

Part of the fun of presents is unwrapping them. You get some clues about what's inside the packaging by the shape and size of the parcel, and its weight. Maybe the parcel rattles. But the excitement grows as you unwrap the parcel and get nearer to the gift. First, the brown paper layer with the address and handwriting, then the gift wrapping and the label – more clues to what's inside. A box next – sometimes anonymous but sometimes more helpful; then tissue paper, and the shop packaging. Inside, at the heart of the parcel, you discover the gift item itself.

It's difficult to unwrap a star, but nevertheless astronomers know quite a lot about what's inside one. The temperature of the surface of the star is one clue – something like the colour of the wrapping paper. The mass and size of the star is another. For instance, if the star is a member of a double-star system, astronomers can look to see how one pulls and passes in front of the other. They can determine the masses and sizes of the star in this way.

We don't hear any rattles from the star, although there *are* things banging around inside stars. Convection currents surge up from the inside of a star, and then fall back, like air currents which make puffy cumulus clouds in Earth's atmosphere. The banging of the surging material inside the star makes sound waves, a rumble of background noise and ringing oscillations as the star resonates like a bell. However, sound doesn't travel across space and we do not hear any of the noises from inside stars.

We do view the radiation from the star's surface. The radiation originates from right inside the star, and the amount of radiation carries messages about what's going on deep in the star's interior, how much energy is being made inside the star, etc. Neutrinos are particles made inside stars and the flux of neutrinos also carries messages from what is inside. At least, neutrinos carry messages about what is inside the Sun, our own star – other stars are too far away for us to detect neutrinos from them.

All these clues show that inside a star is a nuclear reactor. At the star's core, the pressure and the temperature are so high that the nuclei of the atoms of which the star is made bang into each other often and hard, and fuse together into heavier nuclei. They release energy when they fuse together; the energy diffuses to the surface and escapes as radiation; meanwhile, neutrinos given off in the fusion reactions whiz out through the star. The radiation and neutrinos tell us the size of the core and its temperature. The temperature and the pressure of the star keep the star up, and make it the size it is, so astronomers can infer the temperature and density structure throughout the star, not just in the middle.

From these basic data astronomers have calculated the way that stars build up layers inside themselves. Starting with hydrogen as the raw material, the fusion reactions inside stars build up shells of material which has been progressively fused into heavier and heavier nuclei and atoms. At the outer surface of the star is an envelope of unprocessed hydrogen. Inside this envelope is a mantle of helium, and inside this a layer of carbon. In the active core may be a layer of oxygen, neon, calcium. And at the heart of the core, there may be a silicon mixture, burning brightly, fiercely and briefly to make iron.

This is a good story, but how frustrating not actually to see inside a star! It is like guessing what is inside the parcel when the postman delivers it and never actually opening the parcel to confirm the guess!

There are circumstances in which nature unwraps stars for us to see inside. They occur at the end of a star's life. We call these events supernovæ. They represent the blowing up of a star, and its violent disassembly right before our eyes, the layers progressively revealed as the star blows apart. So although astronomers have to wait patiently to unwrap a star, until the right time, the unwrapping day does come, and we can see what's inside.

Astronomers were thrilled to see a star come apart in 1993, progressively revealing what is inside.

The supernova was called SN1993J. It exploded early on March 28, 1993, in the galaxy M81 and was discovered late in the evening by Spanish amateur astronomer Francisco García Diaz. García is a member of the so-called M1 Supernova Search Group of the Madrid Astronomical Association and lives in Lugo in north-west Spain. Over a five-year period, the Group has amassed 25,000 observations of 650 nearby galaxies without finding a single super-nova. But on March 28, with his 10-inch reflector, García saw a 12th magnitude star south of the nucleus of the galaxy M81. It had not been there on March 26. 'I fell off my observing stool and finished the observation on the floor,' he said. It was necessary to check that the star was not the sudden brightening of a variable star in our own Galaxy (there was a nearby confusing fainter star on some charts of M81). After García contacted Jose Ripero, the Group leader, D. Rodriguez confirmed the object with a quick CCD exposure; his colleague P. Pujol estimated its magnitude at 11.3.

It was Ripero who reported the supernova to the International Astronomical Union's Central Bureau for Astronomical Telegrams; he also got in contact directly with colleagues at the Instituto de Astrofísica de Canarias at the telescopes on La Palma, where Enrico Perez took a spectrum the following evening. Alexei Filippenko in Berkeley, California, was also quick off the mark; both spectra confirmed the supernova as a Type II supernova well before maximum light. For groups of astronomers at both these observatories, as well as others throughout the Northern Hemisphere, SN1993J became the focus of attention. For example, it became the most intensely observed supernova in the history of the amateur astronomers' organization, the British Astronomical Association. Professional astronomers on La Palma opened up an electronic database of regular observations of the supernova's magnitude and spectrum.

Further reports followed. R. Kohl of Lakewood, N.Y., spotted the supernova early in the morning of March 31 without having been aware of its prior discovery. J. C. Merlin of Le Creusot in France took an Ektachrome exposure of M81 near midnight on March 27 which was a few hours too early to show the supernova. Unlucky amateur A. Neeley of Silver City, New Mexico took a CCD image about 07.10 UT on March 28 but did not notice the supernova at magnitude 13.8. The International Ultraviolet Explorer satellite, in its fifteenth year as an orbiting astronomical observatory, over-rode its scheduled programme and took spectra of the supernova. The Hubble Space Telescope followed suit.

SN1993J was the closest supernova visible since 1937 for astronomers with Northern Hemisphere equipment. SN1993J is not as close as SN1987A in the Large Magellanic Cloud, visible only to Southern Hemisphere astronomers, but it is a mere 3.3 megaparsecs away (10 million light-years).

SN1993J's parent galaxy, M81, makes a pair with M82 and lies between Alpha and 24 Ursæ Majoris; the two galaxies are separated by the diameter of the Full Moon, and can make a fine sight in a pair

SUPERNOVA 1993J

Daily Means Analysis

Figure 1. The light curve of Supernova 1993J was estimated by amateur astronomer members of the British Astronomical Association and The Astronomer and collected by Guy Hurst of the BAA. The light curve showed a quick rise at the end of March 1993 and fall in the first week of April, and then a slower second maximum which peaked on April 17. After this it faded away, dropping to magnitude 16 at the end of the year.

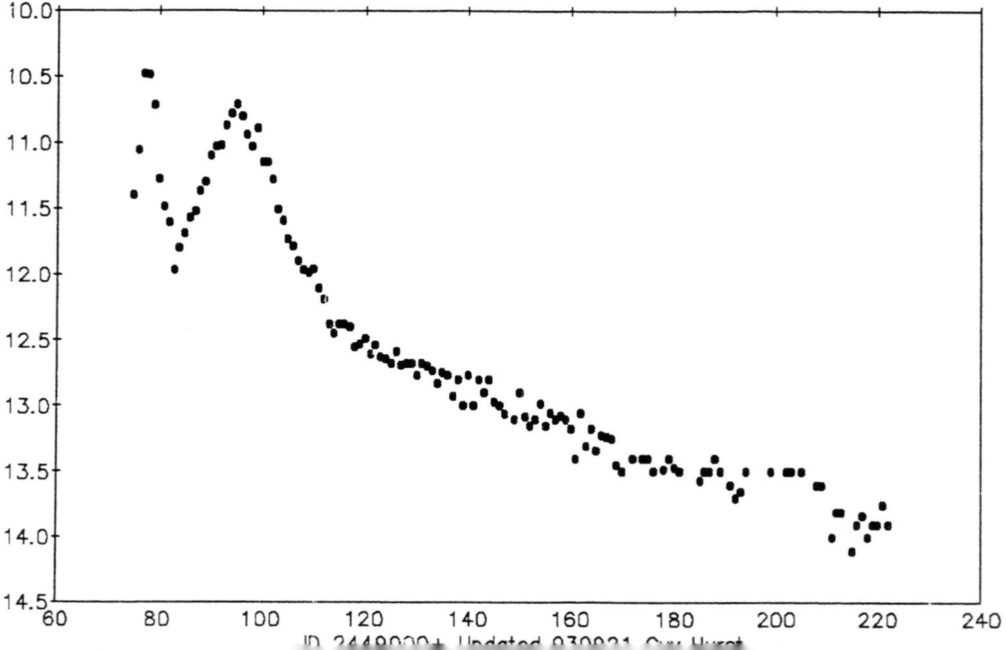

of binoculars on a dark night. Apart from galaxies within the Local Group, M81 and M82 are among the nearest galaxies to the Earth.

What kind of star explodes as a supernova? There are two basic types of supernovæ, and SN1993J was a Type II. A Type II supernova is the sort of supernova which is the explosion of a star at the end of its life. A Type II supernova is an explosion triggered by the collapse, under its own weight, of the iron core which nuclear fusion has built in the centre of a massive star. As the star has shone through its life it has converted hydrogen to helium in the nuclear reactor at its centre. When the hydrogen at the centre of the star is exhausted, the hydrogen-burning zone moves outwards in the star and at the centre the star begins to convert the helium to carbon, for further energy. The carbon is then itself burnt to oxygen, and oxygen burnt to silicon and iron. Eventually the oxygen-burning core is surrounded by shells of carbon-burning, helium-burning and hydrogen-burning material, all inside an envelope of unburnt hydrogen, like successive layers of wrapping paper.

Comes the time when all the oxygen and silicon in the middle of the star is all converted into iron, and there is no more energy-giving fuel left. The flow of energy outwards from the star is what has been all this time supporting the core's weight. When the fuel is exhausted there is no further flow of nuclear energy, and no further support, and the core collapses, suddenly releasing copious amounts of energy which blasts the star apart.

SN1993J was a Type II supernova, with prominent hydrogen lines in its spectrum. The first sign that it was unusual was its light curve. It reached visual magnitude 10.6 on March 31, readily viewable with a small telescope. The total light output from the supernova was weaker than usual for a Type II; moreover, the light curve died away unusually quickly to begin with. About April 5, the supernova had faded to magnitude 12.0.

The explanation for the unusual light curve is that the explosive source at the heart of SN1993J was packed into a very small amount of material. The brightness of a supernova depends on the energy released in the core collapse. This is probably very much the same for all Type II supernovæ, at least if they produce a neutron star, as astronomers suspect is the case for SN1993J. But the brightness also depends on the way that some of this energy is picked up and radiated by the material which is packed around the core. This can vary according to the kind of star which the core is packed in. Apparently the amount of material packed around the core of

(a)

(b)

Figure 2. Nick James (Chelmsford) photographed SN1993J in M81 **(a)** *on April 2, 1993, when it was 10th magnitude, and* **(b)** *again on January 13, 1994, when it had faded to 16th, at the prime focus of his 30 cm f/5.25 reflector.*

SN1993J was rather small, as if the outer envelope of the wrapping was flimsy tissue paper instead of stout brown paper. Because of this, the outer parts of the supernova very quickly started becoming transparent as it expanded. As a result, the supernova released energy in invisible forms, so it looked dim. The amount of exploding material was only some 2.5 solar masses, rather than a more typical value of, say, 10 solar masses.

SN1993J is only the second supernova (after SN1987A) for which the progenitor star has been identified. SN1987A was identified with a *blue* supergiant star Sk-69 202. The progenitor of SN1993J is anonymous, but appears on CCD pictures of M81 made before the explosion, for example from La Palma, Kitt Peak, and the Canada–France–Hawaii Telescope on Mauna Kea. The progenitor of SN1993J has colours which make it appear to be a *red* supergiant, probably a K-type. There is some confusion because the image of the progenitor is elongated and is evidently two stars near the same spot – but they are many light-years separated at the distance of M81, so if they form a double star, it is a very wide pair, with one lazily circling round the other in a very slow distant orbit.

It is much more usual for the progenitor of a Type II supernova to be a red supergiant than a blue supergiant, so SN1993J is more usual in this respect than SN1987A. It is the exact nature of the red supergiant that makes SN1993J out of the ordinary – its mass is too small. Astronomers can account for 4 solar masses in SN1993J (2.5 solar masses of ejecta, 1.5 solar masses in a hypothetical neutron star) but the progenitor is likely to have started as a much more massive star than this, at least 8 solar masses, else it would not have exploded, according to current theories.

Some of this missing material showed itself in early spectra of SN1993J in the form of emission lines which come from circumstellar material – material in the immediate vicinity of the supernova, which presumably came from its progenitor star. From the ground (e.g. the La Palma telescopes), and from satellite-borne ultraviolet telescopes (International Ultraviolet Explorer and the Hubble Space Telescope) astronomers saw evidence of circumstellar material around SN1993J. This material had been surrounding the progenitor star for many millennia, but invisible. When the supernova exploded, the surface of the progenitor star was suddenly heated to extreme temperatures and radiated ultraviolet radiation. This ultraviolet radiation provoked the circumstellar material to shine with emission lines.

The nearby environment produced by the progenitor in its former existence was obliterated by the supernova as it quickly expanded. The interaction between the expanding outer packing and the material of the circumstellar environment caused increasing radio emission from SN1993J, observed by the Ryle Telescope at the Mullard Radio Astronomy Observatory, Cambridge, and by the Very Large Array in New Mexico.

As the ejected material collided with the circumstellar material it also produced soft X-ray emission detected by the Anglo-German X-ray satellite ROSAT only six days after the explosion (the earliest that X-rays have been seen from a supernova), and by the new Japanese satellite Asca (formerly named Astro-D). Asca ('Flying Bird') was launched on February 20, 1993 and SN1993J occurred in the satellite's performance verification phase, during the time the satellite was being tested.

The precise way in which the SN1993J progenitor lost so much of its material to its circumstellar environment is controversial. One theory is that its outer layers were stripped off by a companion star – a much nearer companion star than the one which elongates the progenitor's image. If this is so, we should be able to see the companion when the supernova has faded away enough. The companion may feel a bit the worse for wear, and possibly be speeding off into space from the kick of the explosion, but this will not be visible from such a distance. An alternative theory is that the progenitor was an isolated star of some 20–30 solar masses which had lost more than half of its mass in a stellar wind. Perhaps if we could have seen this star several thousand years ago it would have looked like a Wolf-Rayet star. Wolf-Rayet stars are hot stars with massive wind outflows.

The wind outflow from the progenitor of supernova SN1987A in the Large Magellanic Cloud was not so extreme as the outflow from SN1993J, but nevertheless it happened. We know this because the elliptical ring revealed by the Hubble Space Telescope to lie around SN1987A is the wind outflow material lit up by the light of the explosion; the reason why the material makes such a wonderfully symmetric shape (a circle viewed obliquely) is not known.

Because the progenitor of SN1993J had lost so much of its outer material, by whatever mechanism, expansion of the sparse hydrogen layer of the supernova quickly revealed what lay inside the hydrogen envelope. It was at this stage that astronomers began to see the unwrapping of the star as it came apart.

The nature of the unwrapping process of a star in a supernova explosion is in part like the unwrapping of a parcel by an impatient child, and partly a process special to supernovæ. Just as a child might tear little pieces from the wrappings, to reveal small parts of what lies inside, so the layers of the supernova might crumble into bits, and it becomes possible to see through the gaps between the bits to the interior layers. But also, the layers of supernova are expanding and getting more rarefied. They become transparent and it is possible to see through them to what lies underneath.

The unwrapping of the supernova soon showed the helium shell within the star. The Type II spectrum of SN1993J developed unusually strong helium absorption, and became a Type Ib spectrum. Astronomers believe that this subclass of supernovæ has the same explosive mechanism as Type II but it is packed inside a star which has entirely lost its hydrogen envelope to the circumstellar material. Hydrogen and helium were both visible in the spectrum of SN1993J for a few months.

Late in 1993 SN1993J showed what lay inside the helium shell. Strong oxygen lines in the spectrum indicated that astronomers were seeing deeper into the star to what had been the oxygen-burning layer, a further wrapping below the surface.

There has been one previous case of a Type II metamorphosing into a Type Ib. It was SN1987K observed by Alexei Filippenko of the University of California at Berkeley. The change of SN1987K was incompletely studied as it was behind the Sun at the time of change. A spectrum which Filippenko took before the Sun moved in front of SN1987K was Type II, and the next spectrum, several months later, was Type Ib (unkind astronomers wrongly suggested that Filippenko might have inadvertently confused two separate supernovæ in the same galaxy!). Since SN1993J was close enough for the change to be heralded and since M81 is in a convenient circumpolar constellation, the supernova was closely monitored in order to pin down the change – no chance for confusion this time!

The taking apart of SN1993J has a significant difference from unwrapping a present. You don't expect the act of unwrapping to change the nature of the gift inside the wrapping paper, but this is what a supernova explosion does. The nature of the material inside the core of an exploding star is altered by the explosion.

This was shown by the light curve of SN1993J. In the second week of April 1993, the supernova began to increase in brightness after its initial fade away. A second peak in its light curve occurred about

Figure 3. Martin Mobberley (Bury St Edmunds) recorded SN1993J (arrowed) on April 15, 1993 with his 19-inch f/4.5 Newtonian using a Starlite Express CCD camera. The light from the central disk of M81, inclined at an angle, dominates the central part of the exposure. The supernova sits on a spiral arm of M81 which curves outwards

Figure 4. Harold Ridley (Yeovil) using his 17 cm f/7 Zeiss telescope photographed the galaxies M82 (top), NGC3677 (left) and M81 (bottom) on October 9, 1993 when SN1993J had faded to 14th magnitude (compare with Fig. 2(a)).

towards the bottom of the picture. Apart from the supernova all the other hard round images are stars in our own Galaxy, typically a few thousand light-years away. The supernova, which is in M81 at a distance some 10,000 times further, outshines them all.

April 17 at magnitude 11.0. It is unusual for a supernova light curve to have a second peak. SN1993J has faded steadily since then in a way which is much more normal for Type II supernovæ.

The second peak in the light curve of SN1993J represented the diffusion outwards of energy derived from the radioactive decay of 0.06 solar masses of nickel (Ni-56). This isotope was created by nucleosynthesis in the explosion. The temperatures and densities in the explosion are so enormous that new elements are synthesized in a split second in the core. Some of the elements produced in abundance this way are produced in significant quantities in no other locations in the Universe. Gold is one example – about an Earth-mass of gold was made in the supernova 1993J, to be distributed into the space of M81 for future gold miners to find in whatever planet might form millions of years from now from the outflow.

Ni-56 is significant both because it is produced in quantity and is radioactive. It decays in a matter of a few days into cobalt (Co-56), which is itself radioactive, with a longer half-life. The release of all this radioactive energy takes place near the centre of the explosion where the nickel was created. It takes a couple of weeks for the energy to diffuse up to the surface of the supernova where we can see it. After the initial surge of power reached the surface and things more or less got into in steady state, the light curve of total radiated power from SN1993J showed the characteristic exponential decay rate from the Co-56 isotope.

Astronomy is a passive science, as opposed to an experimental one. Astronomers itch with frustration at not being able to disassemble celestial things to see how they work. SN1993J was a self-disassembly package, and astronomers are still looking in the discarded wrapping paper to see if they have missed any of the items wrapped inside.

The Hunt for Black Holes

PHIL CHARLES

This year has seen renewed interest in the existence of *black holes*, following the suggestion that they could be responsible for the *missing mass* in the Universe. Observations of micro-variability in quasars and the so-called MACHOs in the halo of our Galaxy require large quantities of dark matter in the form of *brown dwarfs* or *black holes* (or anything, so long as it has mass but does not emit light!). But what is the current situation regarding proof of the very existence of black holes? Astronomers now have sophisticated models of the *central engine* that is powering quasars which almost all require the presence of supermassive black holes (typically 10^7–10^9 solar masses). This is because the accretion of matter on to a highly compact object is the most efficient mechanism known for extracting energy, and can therefore explain the quasars' prodigious luminosities. However, just because we cannot think of alternative explanations does not mean that this model is correct! Observations of high velocities very near the centres of active galaxies, and even the dramatic HST images that may have revealed the giant accretion disk surrounding the black hole, are all excellent circumstantial evidence, but they are far from conclusive.

No, our best direct evidence for the existence of black holes has come very recently, and they reside in our own Galaxy. These objects are members of (very) close binaries (double-star systems) and all have one property in common: the companion stars in the binaries are all of low mass and hence are very faint. But how then do we find them? And when we do, how can we be sure that the compact object is a black hole? This is the story of the *hunt for black holes*!

Transient X-ray Outbursts

The brightest X-ray sources in the sky are binary systems, most of which involve neutron stars (recognized by their X-ray pulsations and the X-ray bursts that originate on the neutron star surface). The X-ray luminosity is generated by the transfer of matter from the (normal) companion star on to the compact object. This process is chaotic and leads to substantial variations in the X-ray flux that is produced (indeed if X-rays reached the surface of the Earth, and our eyes were sensitive to them, then the night sky would be a very dramatic display of variations on all time scales, very different from the steadiness of the stars we know). But there is a group of X-ray sources known as *transients* which, as their name implies, undergo massive X-ray outbursts and then fade away during the following months into quiescence, where they remain for as long as ten or twenty years.

It is during these rare outbursts that they are seen by the X-ray cameras on orbiting satellites. The last six years have been particularly fruitful in this area with a succession of missions from Ginga (Japanese), ROSAT (German), GRANAT (Russian) to the Compton Gamma-Ray Observatory (US) all providing some ability to detect such transient sources. But it was Ginga that has so far been the most successful, and the object I want to tell you about was discovered in May 1989 and designated GS2023+338 (which, of course, is simply its approximate position on the sky in RA and dec). Figure 1 shows the X-ray light curve of this source, together with those of several other X-ray transients, showing how they form the class of object that we now know as *Soft X-ray Transients* (the 'soft' refers to the shape of their X-ray spectrum, and corresponds to a lower temperature than that of 'hard' sources).

Now most of these satellites cannot yield a location on the sky of sufficient accuracy to make an optical identification straightforward. It is necessary to go to the telescope as quickly as possible after the X-ray discovery is announced (usually by means of the IAU Circulars) and obtain images of the region of sky containing the X-ray source. These are then compared with archival plates (usually the famous Palomar Observatory Sky Survey) and 'new' stars sought out. But in the case of GS2023+338 it worked out slightly differently. Of course, the Japanese astronomers from Ginga sent the announcement of the source to Brian Marsden (at the Center for Astrophysics, Harvard), who runs the IAU Circulars, but he noticed that the X-ray location was consistent with a previously known variable star, V404 Cygni, and suggested that it might be the counterpart of the new X-ray source. In fact, V404 Cyg is the designation of Nova Cygni 1938 and is contained in well-known catalogues of old novæ. Marsden's suggestion was quickly confirmed when it was found that this star, which is normally around 19th magnitude, had now risen to almost 12th magnitude! This was

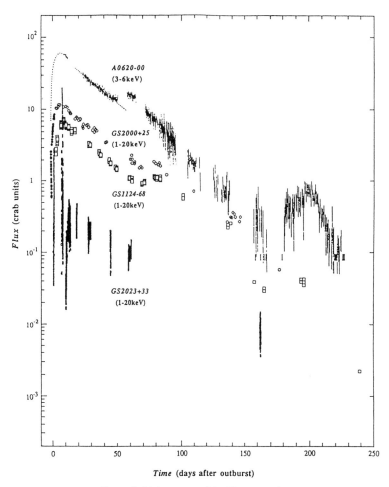

Figure 1. Light curves of the X-ray transients.

the first case of an X-ray transient being identified with a previously known object.

Measuring the Mass

So far all I have pointed out could apply to any of the hundred or so binary X-ray sources that have been found in our Galaxy over the last thirty years. What is it that is special about these transients and enables us to learn so much about the nature of the compact object? The answer lies in Figure 2 which shows schematically one of these systems in outburst and then in quiescence.

In outburst they are (optically) several hundred times brighter than in quiescence, and virtually all of this light comes from the accretion disk which is being irradiated by a massive flux of X-rays. These X-rays 'heat' the disk making it extremely bright and, of course, it is then impossible to see the companion star. But we need to see the companion star if we are to be able to measure its mass, and this is illustrated in Figure 3.

If we can measure the velocity of the companion star in its orbit about the compact object then this gives us the period and the amplitude of the backwards and forwards motion (due to the Doppler effect). Then from Kepler's 3rd Law we can calculate the *mass function* of the system which is defined as

$$(M_x sin\ i)^3\ (M_X + M_C)^2$$

where M_X is the mass of the compact object and M_C is the mass of the companion star (i is the inclination of the orbit to our line of sight). Note what happens in this formula if M_X is very large compared with M_C. If we set M_C to 0 and assume that the inclination is 90° then the mass function is simply M_X, the mass of the compact object itself. This is why this class of X-ray source is so important. We find them through the enormous outbursts they undergo, but when they fade into quiescence the accretion disk is much fainter and we can see the companion star and follow its orbital motion.

This is why it is so difficult to learn about the 'steady' X-ray sources which are luminous all the time. Their accretion disk always dominates the light output from the system and hence the companion star is never visible. Unless we consider *high* mass X-ray binaries such as Cygnus X-1, long thought of as the best candidate for a stellar size black hole. Its problem is that the mass function is actually very low (0.25 solar masses), and this is because the companion star in this binary is itself very massive (a hot, early type OB supergiant). If M_C is large then (as you can tell from the above equation) M_X cannot be determined from the mass function unless M_C is accurately known! There are so many uncertainties and assumptions in this calculation that, all that can be said with confidence, is that M_X is greater than about three solar masses.

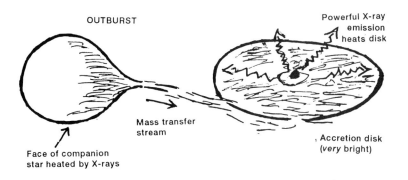

OUTBURST

Powerful X-ray emission heats disk

Mass transfer stream

Face of companion star heated by X-rays

Accretion disk (*very* bright)

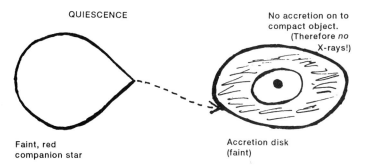

QUIESCENCE

No accretion on to compact object. (Therefore *no* X-rays!)

Faint, red companion star

Accretion disk (faint)

Figure 2. Schematic of an X-ray transient in outburst and quiescence.

Using the WHT on La Palma

By the summer of 1990, V404 Cyg had faded to a visual magnitude of almost 19, and then we turned on to it the power of the 4.2m William Herschel Telescope on La Palma with its newly commissioned spectrograph (ISIS). Together with my Spanish graduate student Jorge Casares (from the Instituto de Astrofísica de Canarias) and British colleague Tim Naylor (University of Keele) our velocity measurements of the companion star revealed the 6.5-day binary period and hence the mass function of 6.1 solar masses. This represents the absolute minimum mass of the compact object. Since we know the system is *not* eclipsing (i.e. the inclination must be less than about 70°) and obviously the companion star mass cannot be 0, then the compact object mass must be **greater** than 6.1 solar masses. We estimate that it must be in the range 7 to 15 solar masses.

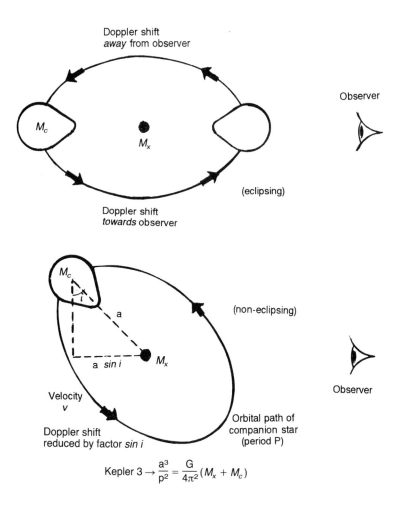

Figure 3. Measuring masses using Kepler's Laws.

Why is V404 Cyg not a Neutron Star?

Until these observations of V404 Cyg were made, the limits on the masses of what were believed to be black hole systems were all around 2 or 3 solar masses. The problem with these results was that they were also consistent with the compact object being a neutron star! How big can a neutron star be? This is a hot topic among theoreticians, but there is quite good agreement that the limit is around 3 solar masses. The solution to this problem is of tremendous importance to theoretical physics because it provides a tight constraint on the equation of state (remember your O-level physics and the perfect gas equation of state?) of matter at the highest densities imaginable (quite impossible to reach using even the most powerful particle accelerators on Earth). In the 1970s, it was shown that, assuming only that General Relativity is correct and that the speed of sound inside the star is less than the speed of light (which means that 'causality' is obeyed), a neutron star could not be more massive than 3 solar masses. Clearly objects at such masses would represent a key test of Einstein's theories.

To be sure that we have found a black hole then we must accurately determine the masses of as many compact objects as possible, searching for those that are significantly above the maximum sustainable neutron star mass. That the object is compact is demonstrated by the powerful X-ray outbursts, and that is why the X-ray transients have been such an important class of object to investigate. The results from the last ten years of observations are summarized in Table 1.

TABLE 1
Observed Properties of Black Hole Binaries

Object	X-ray Luminosity (erg s^{-1})	Distance (kpc)	Spectral Type	V	Orbital Period (days)	Velocity Amplitude (km s^{-1})	Mass Function (M$_\odot$)	Mass (M$_\odot$)
Cyg X-1	2.10^{37}	2.5	O9.7I	9	5.6	76	0.25	>3
A0620-00	10^{38}	1	K5V	12–19	0.32	457	2.91	>3
V404 Cyg	6.10^{38}	2	K0	13–19	6.5	210	6.1	>6

Hence with a **minimum** compact object mass of 6.1 solar masses, V404 Cyg exceeds by a substantial factor the maximum mass of a neutron star, and we are therefore forced to the (conservative!) conclusion that it must be a black hole.

Distortion of the Companion Star

Look again at the schematic of these X-ray binaries in Figure 2. The secondary star is not spherical! Why? The strange pear-shape (known as the *Roche lobe*) is due to the gravitational distortion of the star as a result of the proximity of the compact object. And the more massive the compact object, the greater the distortion. Such a distortion causes a *wave* in the light output from the star and, if measured, can be used to independently determine the mass of the compact object. Essentially the side view of the pear has a larger surface area than the end view and hence is brighter. But since we see both sides during each orbital cycle then we would expect this wave to have *two* maxima and minima per cycle. That is the hallmark of the so-called 'ellipsoidal' modulation which is a result of the intense gravitational distortion of the companion star by the compact object.

As usual, though, this is much harder to put into practice than I have just described. Even during quiescence the accretion disk is still present (although very little if any matter is actually falling on to the compact object itself) and this contaminates the light curve, making it difficult to interpret. The key is to move into the infrared part of the spectrum where the light is dominated by the cool companion star. This is the basis of the approach that Tim Naylor, his graduate student Tariq Shahbaz and I have employed in a study of three of the X-ray transients. But stars of this faintness would have been impossible to observe in the infrared ten years ago. What has transformed the subject is the development in the last five years of infrared arrays which enable true images to be obtained (analogous to CCDs in the optical) and hence much fainter objects can be observed. We have used both UKIRT in Hawaii, and the AAT to obtain IR light curves of Cen X-4, A0620-00 and V404 Cyg. The results on A0620-00 are shown in Figure 4 together with a schematic of the orientation of the binary system.

Combining this observed level of distortion with optical spectroscopy of the companion star enables us to calculate the masses of both stars in the binary, assuming only that the companion star fills its Roche lobe completely (this means that matter at the 'point' of the pear-shape feels an equal gravitational pull from both the compact object and the companion star). For Cen X-4 (which we know to be a neutron star as it produces X-ray bursts) we derive a mass of 1.5 solar masses, in excellent agreement with the expected mass of a neutron star. Whereas for A0620-00 we obtain 10 solar masses! Within the last few months we have obtained similar data on V404 Cyg which yields similar values, but these data are still being worked upon.

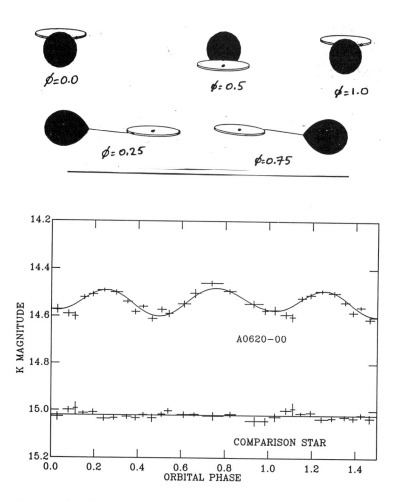

Figure 4. Infrared light curve of A0620-00 obtained with UKIRT (from Shahbaz et al).

Where Next?

Although we have only 2 or 3 black hole 'masses', the results are already very exciting. Whilst neutron star masses (and there are almost a score of them now with very accurate determinations) are all consistent with 1.5 solar masses (and **all** are definitely less than 2 solar masses), the black hole systems are indicating much larger masses. This may well indicate that they are formed in completely different ways and that there is not a continuous mass distribution from neutron stars into black holes. Obviously to confirm this and make substantial progress we need several more systems with accurate masses. We believe we are now within a year or two of being able to make such measurements and enter a new era in our understanding of how black holes are formed and evolve. These results are a testament to the superb observational facilities that UK astronomers now have access to in both hemispheres.

Happy Birthday – Big Eye on the Sky!

RON MADDISON

This year marks the centenary of a most remarkable instrument – the giant 40-inch Refractor at the Yerkes Observatory in Wisconsin, USA.

You may think that I am jumping the gun a little by offering birthday greetings at this time, because the telescope did not actually receive 'first light' until 21 May 1897. But October 1995 is the true centenary of the 40-inch lens, which was beyond doubt the most important part of the instrument – although it turned out to be the second most difficult part of the entire project. As you might expect, the most difficult part was the financing of that enormous telescope.

Those of us who were born more than fifty years ago will remember the few fascinating introductory books on astronomy that were available at that time. In those days, before television and Patrick Moore, they were the only real sources of information and inspiration that steered so many of us eventually into the study of the wonderful and mysterious Universe around us.

Authors such as James Jeans, Harold Spencer-Jones, Norman Lockyer, and Robert Ball readily spring to mind and most of their popular books contain descriptions and pictures of the legendary giant telescopes of the day and were filled with photographs taken with these impressive machines. The largest reflector in the world was then the 100-inch on Mount Wilson in California and the largest refractor was, and still is, the 40-inch refractor at Yerkes. There are very few people who have not seen photographs of these two telescopes.

Refractors

For me, large refracting telescopes have an appeal which reflectors lack and I know that I am not alone in having this preference.

You actually look directly through a refractor along the line of sight to see the object of your study in its true position in the sky.

That seems somehow to make the thing more real. Large refractors are much more convenient to use, and are certainly more æsthetically appealing for visual work than reflectors.

It has been my experience over many years that visitors to an observatory often express their preference for the old reliable 'spy-glass' type of telescope over even larger and more powerful reflectors. I think that this is generally because public demonstration reflectors are more easily abused and knocked out of adjustment than rigidly constructed closed-tube refractors. The open tube reflector seems to be more susceptible to local air currents and dusty mirrors and, as a result, the images lack stability and contrast. It does not help that the cost and labour involved in cleaning and re-surfacing a mirror is so high.

The particular charm of the old Yerkes 40-inch, apart from the fact that it is the biggest of the breed, is its long association with well-known names of the past. When one enters the huge 90-ft diameter dome and stands in the commanding presence of that enormous 63-ft long, 20-ton telescope one cannot help being aware of the generations of astronomers, including almost all of the biggest names in the development of modern astrophysics, who have peered through the eyepiece and perhaps used the instrument in their research.

The fight for light

The story of modern astronomy is essentially the story of the struggle to build bigger and better telescopes, and the steady progress throughout the nineteenth century towards larger apertures was like the progressive breaking of records in the world of athletics.

Although the advance was comparatively small when Roger Bannister broke the previous record in the mile event, his effort is especially remembered because he broke the mystical 'four minute' barrier for the first time. In the same way, the race to build bigger refractors was punctuated by similar mystical targets, and lens diameters seem to have clustered around certain preferred values such as the 12-inch (one foot), the 24-inch (two-foot) and eventually the 36-inch (three-foot). The 40-inch exceeds the one metre barrier.

There is obviously no real significance in this notion, but glass-makers would have set their own targets to make quality blanks as large as the current technology would allow, and they would increase diameters in steps of a few inches each time and try to attain those 'significant' sizes. After all, it is a competitive business and $40 sounds much more than $39.95!

The 36-inch Lick Refractor

The first 36-inch lens was a memorable step. The giant Lick refractor on Mount Hamilton in California was indeed a breakthrough way back in 1888. The lenses for this were cast by Feil and Company in Paris, but the task was almost beyond them, and repeated failures, before final success, led inevitably to their bankruptcy and closure. The blanks were delivered to Alvan Clark, an optician of rare talent; an artist in glass whose instruments are still widely used and can be found all over the world. The engineers of the mounting and observatory were Warner and Swasey, whose names are on so many of the finest telescopes in the world.

The 36-inch was an instant success, which again stimulated the competitive drive to make something even bigger. It was the University of Southern California that took up the challenge and started to make plans for a 40-inch.

At first glance the target increase in diameter of just four inches would seem to indicate political rivalry rather than real scientific advantage as the driving motive. However, if you calculate the improvement in light-gathering area that these extra few inches provide you will see that it represents a 23 per cent increase, which is certainly far from trivial!

The 40-inch and George Ellery Hale

In due course, and with further advances in the art of glassmaking, two blanks of suitable quality were bought by Alvan Clark from Mantois of Paris for the sum of $20,000 – which seems an enormous cost even at current prices, and must have been literally astronomical a century ago!

It is perhaps not surprising that the University soon found that it was unable to proceed with the project and Clark was left holding 'the baby, the bill and all' in what was, in all respects, a very embarrassing situation.

Fortunately the potential disaster was averted when the University of Chicago became involved.

There was a 24-year-old Assistant Professor in the Astronomy Department who was fully aware of what had happened, and realized how much kudos would accrue from taking over the project. He immediately set about finding a solution, and wholeheartedly devoted all his energies to the task of raising sufficient funds to build a telescope to use the 40-inch blanks.

His name was George Ellery Hale. It was no doubt the experience that he gained over the next few years that turned him into the driving force behind the design and construction of all the record-breaking telescopes that were built in the next half century, and culminated in the 200-inch at Palomar that bears his name. That was a series of events that determined the shape of modern astrophysics and is a story for another occasion.

Hale convinced the then President of the University of Chicago, Dr W. R. Harper, of the value of such an acquisition, and between them they finally persuaded Charles T. Yerkes (pronounced: Yurkeez), who had made his fortune with the Chicago trolley-car system, to sponsor the building of the telescope. Hale's lobbying skills and enthusiasm were brought to bear on Yerkes to such great effect that he finally agreed to provide the whole Observatory with all its associated buildings and services – an act of uncommon generosity that cost him over $349,000. It is interesting to reflect that a hundred years later the name of Yerkes is remembered for this fine Observatory and is all but forgotten in the field of trolley-cars.

Figure 1. The main building of Yerkes Observatory. (Photo: Ron Maddison)

Construction and Building

Because of their experience with the 36-inch, Alvan Clark, and Warner and Swasey were given the contract for the 40-inch and construction of that telescope began late in 1892. It was virtually completed by the following summer and maximum publicity was obtained for Yerkes by exhibiting the instrument at the Great Columbian Exposition in Chicago that year.

Meanwhile the Observatory was being built on the low hills of Williams Bay 190 feet above the north shore of Lake Geneva, about eighty miles north-west of Chicago. The site has an elevation of only 1,050 feet above sea level but is well away from any industrial area.

Yerkes Observatory must be the most beautiful observatory in the world.

The old building is set amid beautifully kept gardens and lawns and the building itself is an architectural gem. Three domes are linked by an impressive 'T'-shaped building with the 90-ft dome housing the Great Refractor at the southern end of the long arm. The second dome contains a 41-inch reflector which augments the astrometric work of the refractor by supplying spectrographic radial velocity measurements. The remaining dome houses a 24-inch reflector which is used to test equipment destined for use on larger telescopes at some of the best sites throughout the world.

The stonework, which is described as Romanesque-revival and is a light peach colour is beautifully carved and decorated and has been likened to the Baptistry at Pisa in Italy. The domes themselves have the pale greenish tinge of weathered copper showing through white paint. Half way along each side of the long arm of the 'T' are the front and back entrances each of which is approached via a short flight of steps passing into a colonnaded portico.

I will never forget my first night view of the 40-inch dome as my wife Margaret and I walked in darkness around the eastern wing of the building and saw that beautiful structure lit brightly by a clear first-quarter moon. It stood silently against a myriad of brilliant stars – a silence broken only occasionally by the distant murmur of the motors and wheels as the great dome turned.

The Great Refractor

Inside the building, the south end of the main corridor ends in a long flight of stairs that rise towards a pair of large metal doors that lead directly into the dome housing the Great Refractor. These doors make an effective weather seal that separates the warm

Figure 2. A detail of the view beneath the elevating floor. (Photo: Ron Maddison)

building from what is frequently a sub-zero (Fahrenheit) environment on the other side.

One enters the dome on to a double-fenced catwalk that circles the entire floor area at the lowest observing level. This connects through double gateways to the actual observing floor, which is suspended high above the true ground level by four sets of cables. This entrance level is adjusted so that the eyepiece end of the tube is at a convenient head height when looking near the zenith.

The whole 75-ft diameter observing floor, weighing over 37 tons, can be raised by as much as 23 feet, so that the observer can look with ease at low altitude objects when the telescope is almost horizontal, but at that height the entrance catwalk opens out into the vast empty space under the floor that surrounds the lower half of the massive cast-iron mounting pillar and the heavy stone plinth on which it stands. The entire column extends some 43 feet above ground level, and the reason for the fenced entrance catwalk is very obvious!

On the south side of the telescope pier there is a spiral stairway of three complete turns that gives access to the platform carrying the polar axis. With the floor at the lowest level, this is a daunting climb, but it gives a real appreciation of the true size of the telescope.

Inside the top section of the cast pillar, immediately below the platform, is a small room that houses the drive motors together with the gears and shafting that turn the polar axis. Someone has thoughtfully left a chair there, which I'm sure would be very useful if you had cause to climb to the top very often!

Fate takes a Hand

The major construction work and installation of the telescope was completed in 1897, and preparations were in hand for a dedication ceremony that was to take place in June of that year.

The huge doublet lens, with both glasses weighing some 500lb, arrived in their mounting cell (total weight about half a ton) on 19 May and the fitting and adjustment started immediately. Within two days the telescope was ready for 'first light', and the following few nights were fully occupied in testing and assessing the performance of the new instrument. Numerous resident and visiting experts awaited their turn at the eyepiece, and it was quickly realized that the optical quality was even better than had been anticipated.

Just over a week later, on 29 May, the sky clouded during the late evening and E. E. Barnard and his party of observers retired early. They had been gone for just a few hours when the night watchman

Figure 3. Visitors gather under the Great Telescope for a family portrait in May 1921. The group includes some well-known names from the past. Second from the right is G. Van Biesbroeck. In the centre, eighth from the right, is Albert Einstein. To his right is E. B. Frost, and eighth from the left, at the back, is E. E. Barnard. (Photo: courtesy of Yerkes Observatory)

heard a dreadful crash from the dome that the astronomers had vacated only hours earlier; one of the four pairs of cables supporting the rising floor had come undone, and the whole of the southern end had collapsed and fallen over thirty feet to the ground. This was just a few days before the participants in the dedication were due to walk out on to the floor for the ceremony. Figure 4 shows the débris a few hours after the collapse, and it is most remarkable that the telescope was undamaged, although it must have been severely shaken.

As a result of this accident, which could have been so much worse if it had happened at another time, the floor was redesigned and rebuilt and the dedication was postponed until October 1897. Since

Figure 4. This picture shows the collapsed floor a few hours after it happened in 1897. The pier has been deeply scraped but the telescope is intact. (Photo: courtesy of Yerkes Observatory)

that time it has been a rigid rule that no more than about twenty persons are allowed on to the floor at the same time – which seems to be a very wise precaution.

Attempts to Compete

The great doublet lens has dominated the refractor scene ever since it was completed and we know that it has not been removed from its cell since 1904. This is partly why it is so valuable as an astrometric instrument.

There have been attempts to make larger lenses than the 40-inch, but none was entirely successful. Grubb-Parsons started to make components of 41 inches diameter for a customer in southern Russia, but they were never completed.

A lens of 49.2 inches diameter was successfully completed, and exhibited at the Paris Exhibition of 1900, but it had to be mounted on edge at one end of a fixed horizontal tube and fed by light reflected from an 80-inch diameter siderostat mirror. The whole system was so cumbersome that it was soon dismantled and abandoned.

It is true that many modern Schmidt cameras have correcting

Figure 5. A view of the massive lens with the objective end of the tube tilted downwards. You can see two of the retaining blocks for each of the lenses and the 8-inch air gap ventilated by a total of six oval holes. You can also see the bottom edge of the roller blind dust-cover at the top of its square container. Careful inspection shows the wide open iris diaphragm and several of its edge fixings. (Photo: Ron Maddison)

plates that are bigger even than 49 inches in diameter, but these are generally single pieces of glass having just two almost parallel surfaces.

The present situation is that even with modern materials and techniques, the cost of producing compound lenses has priced the large refractor out of the market – although it is conceivable that future developments might eventually bring them back into favour.

Properties of the 40-inch lens

One of the biggest engineering problems of transparent glass is that it has to be supported from its edge, and in the case of converging, or positive lenses, that is where the material is at its thinnest. For such components most of the weight is concentrated near the centre of the lens and great strain is imposed on the thin supporting rim. The surfaces distort and good optical performance is lost.

The following dimensions of the 40-inch lens may be of interest:

It is an air spaced achromatic doublet made from crown and flint glasses.

Figure 6. A close-up picture of the edge of the lens showing the ⁵/₁₆-inch hole that was drilled at the head of a small crack to stop any further growth. The immediate area is masked by a small rectangular light stop. (Photo: Ron Maddison)

The positive outer crown component has a central thickness of 2.5 inches and an edge thickness of 0.7 inch.

The negative inner flint component has a central thickness of 1.5 inches and a probable edge thickness in excess of 3 inches. The two components are separated by 8.4 inches, and the air gap is ventilated by six large oval openings cut through the cell wall.

The focal length of the combination is 63.5 feet (762 inches), giving an 'f' ratio of 19.05.

The only serious disturbance to the lens that may have caused problems occurred in the exceptionally cold winter of 1977.

Figure 7. This is a stereo pair of pictures that reveal the huge size of the telescope and dome. The pictures can be viewed without a stereoscope by holding them about a foot in front of your face and relaxing your eyes as if you were focusing on a distant horizon. The pictures will gradually blend together as your eyes diverge and you look at the right one with the right eye, and the left one with the left eye. As a result you will see three pictures in a line. You may need to tilt both pictures slightly to get a perfect blend, but the central picture is the fully three dimensional view. If you are unable to do this you should be able to see them more easily with a stereoscope. (Photos: Margaret Maddison)

A routine inspection, carried out in February of that year revealed a fine radial crack at the edge of the outer component that was just under half an inch long. The crack was located at one of the three outer retaining blocks that prevents the lens from moving in its cell and it was thought that the excessive cold may have caused mechanical compression at this point.

In September 1977 the lens was rotated by 18° to bring the fault clear of the retaining block, and the glass was examined in polarized light to look for any residual stress. When, as expected, none was found it was decided to prevent any further problem by drilling a five-sixteenths of an inch diameter hole through the lens at the head of the crack. This was done with the lens still in its cell – a remarkable feat in its own right – and there has been no detectable effect on the performance of the telescope since that time.

As I write these notes (January 1994) the Lake Geneva area in Wisconsin is again experiencing record-breaking low temperatures, lower even than those in 1977, and I'm sure that we all hope that no further damage will be caused.

The End of an Era?

At a time when the Hubble Space Telescope is now working at full power and multi-metre reflectors are being assembled on high mountain sites around the world, you may wonder if there is still room for these old relics of the past.

In truth, old refractors actually improve with age. This is because the thin patina-like layer that is formed on the lens surface by oxidation and corrosion acts like the blooming on all modern lenses. It reduces surface reflection and promotes better transmission of light through the glass.

But there is still much useful work to be done by what are now regarded as relatively small instruments. This is not the headline making, blockbusting discovery work that can only be done with state-of-the-art newly developed equipment – but the routine measurement and classification work that is so fundamentally important in the study of the unimaginably vast volume of material that surrounds us.

In any case the 40-inch is a most important part of our astronomical heritage and I wish it well as it begins its second century.

Happy birthday, Big Eye on the Sky!

Cataclysmic Variables from Origin to Outburst

CHARLES GORDON-GRAHAM

Introduction

Looking into the night sky, you see thousands of stars, and (apart from the atmospheric phenomenon of twinkling) their brightness is steady. As far as European astronomers, a few centuries ago, were concerned that was how it had to be: the stars did not change. Yet if you look again over the following few nights, you may notice that some of those stars do indeed vary in brightness. As you study these *variable* stars over time you find patterns that emerge, and you can group variable stars together into types that exhibit similar behaviours. Some are regular, some are irregular, and some again take the middle way, being semi-regular.

Variable stars come in all masses, sizes, and luminosities. Some of the most famous stars are variable, such as Betelgeux, the Pole Star, and even our closest stellar neighbour, the Sun. There are *eclipsing binaries*, and there are pulsating stars such as *Mira* stars and *Cepheids*. There are *flare stars*, and there are *magnetic variables*, noted for their anomalous spectra as well as their strong magnetic fields.

The most spectacularly variable stars are the *supernovæ*, known as 'guest stars' by the classical Chinese astronomers who observed them. Their world view admitted change in the heavens – indeed change is an essential part of their understanding of the Universe. Thus they had no qualms about recording observations of stars that suddenly appeared in the night sky, as if from nowhere, to outshine all the other stars, remaining visible for months, even in broad daylight, before gradually fading once again into obscurity. Of these, the most famous is that of 1054, since identified as the progenitor of the Crab Nebula and its pulsar. There are also Korean, Japanese, and Arabian records of supernovæ, and it seems that American Indians have also witnessed such phenomena. Supernovæ were observed in Europe by such eminent astronomers as Tycho Brahe and Kepler, at a time when old assumptions about the heavens were being seriously challenged. But such stupendous outbursts are rarely seen – none has been observed in our Galaxy since 1604, though they have been studied in other galaxies, using sophisticated equipment.

And then there are the *cataclysmic variables*, of which about three or four hundred are known, and it is they that form the subject of this article. Maybe they are not quite as dramatic as supernovæ – they don't outshine a whole galaxy during outburst – but they are still very impressive in their own right, and worthy of the attention of the many professional and amateur astronomers around the world who study them.

In the literature they are sometimes referred to as *cataclysmic binaries*, since they are close binary systems of low mass, typically consisting of a 'normal' main sequence or giant star transferring mass to its compact companion, either a white dwarf, sub-dwarf or neutron star. Matter may flow via an accretion disk or be channelled to the compact star along magnetic field lines, depending on the latter's magnetic field. In the next section we shall discuss the basic observational data and the different classes of cataclysmic variable.

Observations and Classification

The orbital periods of cataclysmic variables are less than a day, in most cases between 80 minutes and 12 hours. There is also a period gap observed: hardly any cataclysmic variables are known with periods between 2 and 3 hours, a point that we shall discuss later. The period could be less than 80 minutes if both stars are degenerate or if the secondary is helium rich (making it smaller than a normal main sequence star). In those systems with periods greater than 12 hours the secondary is an upper main sequence or a sub-giant star and the primary a neutron star (or even a black hole?).

Cataclysmic variables are grouped into several classes, some of which are characterized by outbursts, which may occur in the disk or on the surface of the compact star. The parameters that distinguish the various types of cataclysmic variable include the character of the component stars, orbital period (and separation), mass transfer rate, magnetic field, and the source of outburst. We shall now describe the various classes in a little more detail.

Classical novæ are characterized by high mass transfer rates and outbursts (sometimes themselves called novæ) where the system brightens by between 9 and 14 magnitudes in just one or two days and fades over tens or hundreds of days, and a shell is ejected (some novæ have been found to shed more than one shell). In quiescence most of the light comes from the accretion disk.

Similar to the classical novæ are the *recurrent novæ*, which have a higher mass transfer rate from the secondary, which is in this case a giant star. The outburst amplitude is 7 to 9 magnitudes, less than for a classical nova, but outbursts are observed every ten to a hundred years. The giant star is the main source of light during quiescence.

Dwarf novæ undergo frequent outbursts, with a recurrence time of 10 to 500 days. The outburst amplitude is 2 to 6 magnitudes. The absolute magnitude of a dwarf nova in outburst is comparable to that of a classical nova in quiescence. It seems that the main source of light during quiescence is a hot spot on the disk. Mass transfer rates are lower than for classical or recurrent novæ. Dwarf novæ are subdivided into three types. In outburst *U Geminorum stars* ('classical' dwarf novæ) brighten faster than they fade, though for any one system the time it takes to return to quiescence varies from between 5 and 20 days. *Z Camelopardalis stars* are noted for their standstills. They go through periods, sometimes for years, without undergoing outbursts. The brightness at standstill is about the same at each standstill and is about the same as the average brightness over the normal light curve (quiescence and outburst). *SU Ursæ Majoris stars* experience supermaxima in addition to normal outbursts, the supermaxima being more regular. It is believed that their light curves are also affected by tidal distortion of the secondary.

There are also related systems with higher mass transfer rates than those in dwarf novæ, but which are not observed to undergo outbursts. Such *novalike variables* are subdivided into *UX Ursæ Majoris stars*, which resemble old novæ photometrically and spectroscopically but apparently show less violent flickering, and *VY Sculptoris stars*, whose spectra resemble those of dwarf novæ in outburst, and whose behaviour photometrically is similar to that of SU UMa systems, with occasional deep minima which can continue for weeks or months, perhaps due to a drop in mass transfer rate.

In contrast to the classes of cataclysmic variable discussed so far, there are the *magnetic systems*, where the white dwarf has a magnetic field strong enough significantly to affect the mass transfer process. There are two subclasses, the *AM Herculis stars*, sometimes referred to as *polars*, and the *DQ Herculis stars*, also known as *intermediate polars*. (There is, however, some debate as to whether the prototype DQ Her itself belongs to this subclass!) In AM Her systems the white dwarf's magnetic field is great enough to prevent an accretion disk from forming at all. Instead, matter is transferred through an accretion funnel or column on to one or both magnetic poles of the white dwarf. In DQ Her systems the white dwarf's magnetic field is not as strong as in the AM Her systems, so that an outer accretion disk is able to form, but otherwise the two sub-classes are similar.

Symbiotic stars were discussed by David Allen in an article in an earlier *Yearbook*. These are now believed to be detached systems consisting of a red giant and a sub-dwarf. It seems that there is indirect mass transfer from the giant star through a stellar wind. *Cataclysmic low mass X-ray binaries* are characterized by their strong and variable X-ray emission. Here the compact star is not a white dwarf but a neutron star. In *double degenerate systems* both stars are compact: for example, they may both be white dwarfs. An example is AM Canum Venaticorum, whose period is only 17 minutes.

The spectrum of a cataclysmic variable at quiescence typically includes a fairly blue optical continuum with a significant ultraviolet component, fairly broad and strong hydrogen emission lines, weak emission lines from helium and ionized calcium, and X-ray emission. Weak absorption lines, presumably from the red dwarf, are also observed. A further element is sometimes found, called the S wave, emanating from the region where the stream from the secondary star collides with the outer part of the disk producing the hot spot, though a recent study of some nova-like variables anomalously did not reveal any S waves.

In a dwarf nova outburst the optical flux increases, with a time delay before the ultraviolet flux grows, though they fade together. At outburst the hard X-ray flux increases at most moderately, and can even decrease. During early rise the emission lines disappear, as do the absorption lines from the red dwarf, and are replaced by weak, broad absorption lines that dominate the spectrum at maximum. The spectrum resembles that of an A-type star during the rise, and a B-type star at maximum. During early decline this process is reversed, the emission lines re-appearing again, until by mid-decline the spectrum becomes once again like that at quiescence. The exact pattern varies from one dwarf nova to another, but different outbursts of any one dwarf nova are very similar.

Infrared emission has been detected at outburst from the brightest of the U Gem stars, SS Cygni, though not from some other cataclysmic variables studied at the same time. It is likely that the infrared emission is due to the heating of circumstellar dust by the enhanced ultraviolet flux during outbursts. Ultraviolet observations reveal a P Cygni type line profile at outburst, consisting of broad emission and highly blue-shifted absorption components, implying a stellar wind at this time. The circumstellar dust may have condensed from material ejected in several outbursts.

In nova outbursts the spectrum resembles that of a supergiant A-type star during the rise, suggesting that the enormous increase in luminosity is due to a huge expansion in the light-emitting surface of the system, rather than to an increase in temperature. During the decline, Cepheid-like fluctuations are often observed, and as the broad emission lines re-appear they are Doppler shifted as a shell is ejected at about 2000 kilometres per second. In some cases, such as Nova Aquilæ 1918, the expansion of the shell has been recorded photographically, which provides a tool for determining the distance of the nova.

At this point it might be worth mentioning that the star P Cygni was recorded as a nova in 1600 and again in 1606 – nearly four centuries later its spectrum shows the star to be continuously ejecting an envelope. One may also cite the Wolf–Rayet stars, characterized by their extremely broad emission lines. Some astronomers believe that these stars are shedding mass at velocities up to 3000 kilometres per second, at which rate they would lose their entire mass in two or three million years, a mere blink in the aeons of cosmic time. About half of the known Wolf–Rayet stars are in binary systems.

In addition to outbursts, other forms of variability are observed in cataclysmic variables, such as orbital modulation (physical, as well as geometrical) and flickering in optical and X-ray emission over time scales of minutes, perhaps originating in the hot spot. Rapid oscillations over tens of seconds are also observed, for which explanations include rotating hot spots on the disk or white dwarf, instabilities in the accretion flow and non-radial pulsations in the disk or on the surface of the white dwarf.

Various photometric and spectroscopic techniques have been employed in the study of cataclysmic variables, of which two recent developments are *eclipse mapping* and *Doppler tomography*. In eclipse mapping the light curve is compared with the predictions of the theoretical model, whose parameters are then adjusted to fit the observed data. This model-fitting approach is constrained by some gaps in our knowledge of accretion disk theory, so an image reconstruction method has been devised which treats the intensity at each point on the disk surface as an independent parameter. This technique has been described by Horne. Together with Marsh, he has also written about the related method of Doppler tomography, in which the shape of the emission line profile is analysed in detail. For example, a hot spot on the disk will show up as an enhanced intensity hump whose wavelength (and thus relative position within the line profile) will change due to the variation in its Doppler shift as it orbits around the compact star. Both techniques have been powerful observational tools and provide opportunities to test the theoretical models, to which we shall now turn.

Theoretical Models of Behaviour

In the literature close binary stars are often described in terms of Roche geometry. We shall draw an analogy which is often used when discussing the idea of curved space-time in the general theory of relativity, namely that of a sheet of rubber whose shape is distorted by the presence of balls placed on it. The more massive the ball, the more it stretches the rubber and the deeper the well it forms. One may pour water into such a well, but there may come a time when the water fills the well and spills over.

The gravitational field of a star may then be regarded as a well, which is called the *Roche lobe* of that star. The greater the total mass of the star, the greater the size of its Roche lobe. For most of its life a star will remain easily within its Roche lobe, but when it reaches the red giant stage its envelope expands enormously and material spills over out of the Roche lobe in the form of a stellar wind or may be ejected as a planetary nebula.

In a close binary each star occupies a well, whose shape is modified by the existence of the other star, and from a distance the system behaves like one larger well. The proximity of the two stars may result in a star filling its Roche lobe due to the gravitational field of its companion, regardless of the evolutionary state of the star, and material then spills over and enters the companion star's Roche lobe. Transfer of material from a less to a more massive star leads to an increase in the separation of the stars, which will lead to the mass transfer being cut off, unless there is some force to prevent this expansion of the binary. Possible forces driving mass transfer and their impact on the evolution of cataclysmic variables will be considered later.

Having provided a simple analogy for the Roche geometry, we

shall discuss the *canonical model* (see Figure 1) in more detail. The main sequence or giant secondary fills its Roche lobe and matter flows into an accretion disk (except in the strongly magnetic systems, which will be discussed shortly), forming a hot spot where it meets the disk. Material then spirals inwards, being heated as it does so due to friction with neighbouring layers. In old novæ and nova-like systems with their high mass transfer rates, the disk temperature is around 8000 K and the material is optically thick (i.e. opaque). For dwarf novæ, where the mass transfer rate is lower, the disk is optically thin and at a temperature of around 4000 to 5000 K, virtually independent of the radial distance from the white dwarf. Irradiation of the secondary star by both the disk and the white dwarf is believed to be significant, and Smak has discussed irradiation of the disk itself, arguing that the emission lines of ionized helium can be explained by photo-ionization, in this case ionization of disk material by X-rays from the boundary layer between the disk and the white dwarf.

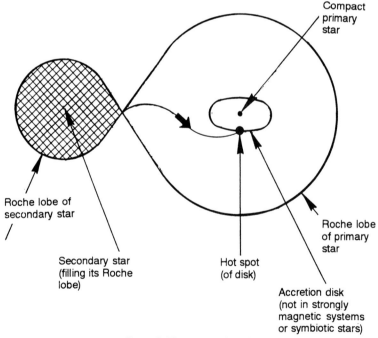

Figure 1. The canonical model.

However, there are a number of uncertainties in accretion disk theory, such as the exact source of the observed emission lines, the precise extent of irradiation of the disk, and the absence of S waves for some nova-like variables. Observational work by Dhillon *et al* shows that additional factors must be considered, such as magnetic curtains and accretion disk winds (like a tenuous corona), in order to explain the line emission, though detailed calculations have yet to be made on these effects.

Before describing outburst mechanisms, we shall now turn our attention to the strongly magnetic systems, the AM Her stars, where there is no accretion disk. Here the accretion flow is governed by the white dwarf's magnetic field which channels material on to one or both magnetic poles (one of which is stronger), and a shock is formed near the surface of the white dwarf. It is believed that the white dwarf in these systems rotates synchronously with the orbit, which probably requires the secondary star itself to have a surface magnetic field. Theoretical studies show that synchronization is easier if the white dwarf's mass is less than about 0.6 solar masses. Furthermore, it seems that such systems would be unstable with periods above four hours, in accordance with the observed short periods (mostly below the period gap).

Campbell has attempted to explain the observed low states in the strongly magnetic systems by suggesting that there is a small asynchronism, which will lead to changes in the geometry of the system. He finds certain orientations of the white dwarf that seem to restrict the mass transfer, and as the white dwarf passes through these restrictive orientations it will go through phases of reduced accretion for a few months – the duration of the observed low states. In any case, it is hard to explain the magnetic behaviour of these systems unless most of their luminosity is in the extreme ultraviolet and soft X-ray spectrum, which is observed in some cases.

In contrast to the AM Her stars, in intermediate polars an outer accretion disk forms, but closer to the white dwarf it is the latter's magnetic field that directs the accretion flow. In these systems, whose orbital periods place most of them above the period gap, the spin period is typically a tenth of the orbital period (except DQ Her itself, where the spin period is about a hundredth of the orbital period). One would expect that intermediate polars will evolve into AM Her systems as the orbital period decreases, along the lines of the common envelope evolution theory outlined later.

We shall now consider the outburst mechanisms in dwarf novæ

(see Figure 2). It seems that what drives the accretion flow through the disk is viscosity. Its effect is to reduce the mass flow rate through the disk, so that as mass enters the disk it piles up, and thus the surface density of material in the accretion disk increases. At this stage the disk is cool and convective, but there comes a time when the surface density is too high for this to remain a stable state for the disk, and there is a sudden and explosive flip to a hot radiative state.

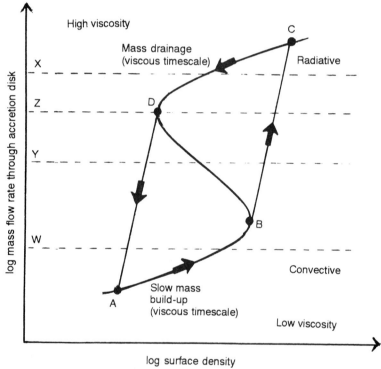

Figure 2. Mass transfer rates in accretion disks.

W = Low mass transfer rate from secondary star – stable.

X = High mass transfer rate from secondary star – stable (e.g. old novæ, nova-like variables).

Y = Intermediate mass transfer rate from secondary star – unstable and prone to regular outbursts (e.g. classical dwarf novæ).

Z = Fairly high mass transfer rate from secondary star – marginally stable: prone to regular outbursts interspersed with periods of approximately constant brightness (e.g. Z Cam systems).

Following this there is a net draining of material from the accretion disk as the flow rate through the disk is now greater than the mass transfer rate from the secondary star to the disk. Thus the surface density falls again, but then it reaches a point where the disk can no longer remain hot and radiative, so it jumps back to a cool convective state, with a consequent decrease in luminosity until it stabilizes again. This process repeats as the system follows the course of this hysteresis loop.

The mass transfer rate from the secondary is higher for old novæ and nova-like variables than for dwarf novæ, high enough for the disk to remain in the hot radiative state all the time, and thus these stars do not undergo the outbursts described above. Conversely, in systems with mass transfer rates significantly lower than those for dwarf novæ the disk remains in the cool convective state and for that reason outbursts do not occur. Z Cam stars are borderline, their mass transfer rates being at the critical threshold value, so that these systems go through phases where they are subject to outbursts interspersed with the observed standstills.

A nova outburst is believed to be due to a thermonuclear runaway, similar in this respect to a supernova outburst, though a different process is involved, and it is probably a recurring phenomenon even for the classical novæ (with a frequency of perhaps ten thousand years). As matter accretes on to the white dwarf it forms a layer, which becomes hotter and hotter, since the degeneracy pressure which holds up a white dwarf star against its gravity does not allow the gas to expand and cool. Once enough of this hydrogen-rich material has collected on the surface of the white dwarf, the temperature and pressure become so high as to enable thermonuclear fusion of hydrogen to helium to start. This releases an enormous amount of energy, which heats the gas still further, and because the gas still cannot expand and cool a runaway process ensues, culminating in the observed eruption – one or more shells being ejected, containing perhaps a ten-thousandth of a solar mass, a little more than the white dwarf gained by accretion from the secondary.

Since the mass transfer rate for recurrent novæ is greater it takes less time for the white dwarf to acquire enough material for such a thermonuclear runaway, and less mass may be required. As a result, eruptions are seen more frequently, though the energy released is less than for classical novæ. The existence of a giant secondary also means that the system is intrinsically much brighter at quiescence, so that is a further factor in the smaller outburst amplitude observed compared with classical novæ.

Origin and Evolution

We now turn to the issues of the origin and evolution of cataclysmic variables and of their place within the Universe. It is estimated that there are between 30 and 50 novæ per year in the Milky Way and about the same in similar galaxies. Cataclysmic variables are found in the old disk of the Galaxy, so that by galactic standards they are of intermediate age, like the Sun.

One would expect low mass binaries – i.e. potential or actual cataclysmic variables – to be very common, since maybe half of all stars are found in binary systems, and the majority of stars are of lower mass than the Sun, itself a lightweight compared to some. However, they would be hard to detect, since, apart from the occasional giant component such stars would be quite faint. For example, our nearest stellar neighbour after the Sun is α Centauri, consisting of a primary star very like the Sun, together with a K-type dwarf secondary and an M-type dwarf. Yet despite being a mere 4.3 light-years away, this system only appears as the third brightest star in the night sky as seen from Earth. Indeed Proxima Centauri, the smallest – and closest – component, is invisible without a telescope!

One might infer that many binary stars experience a cataclysmic variable phase of their evolution, so long as at least the primary is massive enough to become a red giant at some stage. Moreover, there must also be a means for wide binaries to lose angular momentum (a quantity that depends on the masses and orbital and spin velocities of the stars, and on their separation) – they must shed enough in order to evolve into close binaries with separations of about two solar radii. What follows is the *common envelope evolution* theory, which provides a broad picture of our understanding of the origin and life history of a cataclysmic variable.

According to this theory, the two stars evolve independently until the primary exhausts its core hydrogen and becomes a red giant. The primary expands to fill its Roche lobe and there is a rapid mass transfer to the secondary. The time scale of this accretion is much shorter than the time scale for the secondary to re-adjust thermally to its increased mass, and the star becomes engulfed by the envelope of the primary, so that there is now a common envelope, which is then ejected, leading to a loss of mass and angular momentum from the system. With this loss of angular momentum the system is left as a close binary made up of a white dwarf and a red star with an orbital period of a day, surrounded by the ejected shell. It is believed that planetary nebulæ are the ejected envelopes of former red giants, their core stars being small, hot sub-dwarfs or Wolf–Rayet stars on their way to white dwarfhood, and observations of one planetary nebula indeed reveal a close binary containing an O-type sub-dwarf and a probable M-type dwarf with a separation of two solar radii. Further angular momentum loss then results in the system having a period of about half a day, as typically observed for cataclysmic variables. This could perhaps be achieved through magnetic braking, involving the interaction between the magnetic fields of the primary star and of the interstellar medium.

The secondary star has not been able to re-adjust thermally to its new circumstances, and is oversized for its mass and fills its Roche lobe, thus transferring material to the compact primary. Magnetic braking could continue to drive the mass transfer, but as the system shrinks, it becomes a weaker effect, until the orbital period is down to three hours, when the secondary star is then able to re-adjust to its reduced mass and shrink within its Roche lobe, cutting off mass transfer. Once the period has reduced to two hours, gravitational radiation has become strong enough to drive mass transfer, which thus resumes, again too fast for the secondary to re-adjust thermally. This continues until a minimum period is reached, after which the dynamics dictate an increase in the period again, cutting off mass transfer once more, leaving the primary white dwarf to cool down and the secondary to evolve probably to become a brown dwarf.

There is also the *hibernation theory*, according to which cataclysmic variables alternate between periods of increased mass transfer, behaving as novæ, and periods of reduced mass transfer, during which they behave as dwarf novæ. This sounds an appealing idea, but as yet no clear reason has been established for the alternation in the mass transfer rate.

It is estimated that at an occurrence of 30 to 50 outbursts a year the total amount of material ejected by novæ in the Galaxy is comparable with that ejected by supernovæ. Some of the material of which we ourselves are made may once have been inside a red dwarf star, lost to a white dwarf companion and ejected into the interstellar medium through a nova outburst – in such a way is the Universe inter-connected.

There are many questions yet to be answered about cataclysmic variables. We have already mentioned the uncertainties concerning accretion disk behaviour. We could also ask what exactly are the relationships of cataclysmic variables (if any) with planetary nebulæ, Wolf–Rayet and P Cygni stars? How does one apply the common envelope theory to systems where the secondary is a giant, as in the recurrent novæ? In this case, what would happen to the envelope of the giant as it expands as though to engulf the system, bearing in mind that the primary is a white dwarf? A further puzzle arises from recent indications that secondary stars may actually be sub-giants rather than main sequence stars. And what about Nova Cygni 1975, now believed to be an AM Her star – how does the presence of a strong magnetic field affect a nova outburst? These are some of the outstanding issues in this exciting area of astronomy.

References
Campbell, C. G., 1984, *Mon. Not. R. astr. Soc.*, 211, 83

Dhillon, V. S. *et al*, 1992, 'An Observational Study of the Eclipsing Novalike Variable B H Lyncis (= PG 0818+513)'

Gordon-Graham, C., 1985, 'Mass Transfer in Cataclysmic Binaries'

Hoffmeister, C., Richter, G., and Wenzel, W., 1985, 'Variable Stars', Springer Verlag

Horne, K., 1985, *Mon. Not. R. astr. Soc.*, 213, 129

Jameson, R. F. *et al*, 1987, *The Observatory*, Vol 107, No 1077

King, A. R., 1988, *Mon. Not. R. astr. Soc.*, Vol 29, No 1

Marsh, T. R. and Horne, K., 1988, *Mon. Not. R. astr. Soc.*, 235, 269

Pringle, J. E. and Wade, R. A. (editors), 1985, *Interacting Binary Stars*, Cambridge University Press

Smak, J., 1992, 'Emission Lines from Accretion Disks in Cataclysmic Variables', review presented at the Vulcano Workshop (Italy)

Wood, J. H. and Horne, K., 1990, *Mon. Not. R. astr. Soc.*, 242, 606

Acknowledgements to Dr R. C. Smith at the University of Sussex for our interesting discussions.

Astronomy's Multi-Fibre Revolution

FRED WATSON

It looks for all the world like a length of nylon fishing-line, or perhaps the top E-string of a classical guitar. It is quite flexible – you can tie a knot in it – and its breaking strain, though not enough to land a 10-lb pike, is surprisingly high. Yet this fine strand of man-made material has an almost magical property that sets it apart from its humbler cousins. A beam of light entering one of its ends will emerge, virtually undiminished, at the other. It is, of course, an optical fibre – a modest miracle of technology that encompasses within its microscopic diameter a perfectly formed ring-structure of different types of glassy fused silica. Embedded in a thicker protective sheath of plastic material, the slender fibre takes on the workaday appearance that belies its true nature.

It is the very high transparency of the silica, together with the perfection of the boundary between the different layers, that allows light to bounce along inside the fibre over distances that may amount to tens of kilometres – given a long enough strand. Such 'low-loss' optical fibres were developed for communications purposes, to allow the long-distance transmission of messages along beams of light in much the same way as telephone wires use currents of electricity, but with vastly greater efficiency. Since its infancy in the early 1970s, the optical communications industry has progressed rapidly, and a growing fraction of the world's communications is now handled by fibre optics.

Fibre optics in astronomy

It was almost two decades ago that the fertile mind of an expatriate British scientist, working at the Steward Observatory in Arizona, dwelt on the possibilities of fibre optics for astronomy. Dr Roger Angel is, perhaps, now better known for his invention of the spin-casting technique that will furnish some of the coming generation of giant telescopes with their mirrors. In 1977, though, recognizing that optical communications engineers guard their photons against loss as jealously as astronomers do, he saw that optical fibres could have a bright future in astronomy.

The first application he suggested was in an ambitious super-telescope, to be formed by linking together a hundred 2.5-metre diameter telescope mirrors by means of fibre optics. The idea was that every mirror would have a fibre at its focus, so that pointing all the mirrors toward the same celestial object would allow the incoming light to be combined by bringing the fibres to a single point. Here they would feed a spectrograph – that indispensable weapon in the astronomer's armoury that allows the faint light of stars, galaxies and quasars to be analysed to reveal hidden vital statistics. The 100 mirrors together would form the equivalent of a 25-metre telescope, and thus allow the observation of very much fainter objects than is possible with existing instruments.

Doubtless, you will have noticed that this super-telescope has not, so far, materialized. However, Angel's next idea for fibre optics certainly has. Indeed, the technique is now proliferating through the world's major observatories, quietly revolutionizing the way in which astronomical spectroscopy is carried out.

Curiously, it is a kind of inverse of his first scheme. Instead of using fibres to join a spectrograph to several telescopes looking at a single object, they are used to bring light from several objects in the field of view of a single telescope to the spectrograph. Because of the way spectrographs are made, all these objects can be observed

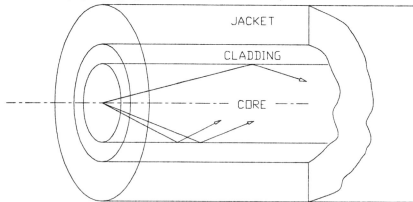

Figure 1. Internal structure of a typical optical fibre suitable for astronomy. Some of the paths taken by light rays from an image in the centre of the input-face are shown. The core and cladding are made from different types of glass-like fused silica, and the light is guided along the core by repeated reflections at the interface. Surrounding the cladding is a protective jacket, made from a polymer such as nylon or acrylate. Core diameter is typically around 0.1 mm, while the jacket might be anything up to 0.5 mm.

simultaneously if they can be lined up on the entrance slit of the instrument. That is where the flexibility of the fibres comes in – they are used to rearrange (or *re-format*) the random pattern of target objects in the telescope's field of view into a neat row. Thus, astronomers can choose which objects they want to observe, align a fibre to intercept the light from each one, and look at them all simultaneously with the spectrograph.

The net result is that the spectrum of each object (its light split into component rainbow colours) is aligned neatly alongside its neighbour to form a stack of spectra that can be detected with a CCD – the sensitive TV-type camera that is among the modern astronomer's most useful tools. Since the normal way of capturing the detailed spectra of celestial objects is one at a time, the big improvement here lies not in the faintness of the objects that can be observed, but in the *efficiency* with which data on large numbers of objects can be collected. Angel recognized that the potential for such a system was very high. Imagine being able to point a telescope towards a cluster of galaxies and obtain redshifts (the spectral signature that indicates velocity) of all of them simultaneously. Or to be able to obtain detailed information about dozens of stars in a globular cluster in one observation. The saving on that most precious of the astronomer's commodities – telescope-time – would be enormous.

'Medusa' and her descendants

It was left to one of Angel's postgraduate students to meld these ideas into a practical proposition. Working with colleagues at the University of Arizona, John Hill developed an optical fibre system for the Steward Observatory's 2.3-metre telescope at Kitt Peak. It was built specifically for the determination of cluster galaxy redshifts, and was eventually highly successful, winning for Hill the prestigious Trümpler Award of the Astronomical Society of the Pacific.

At the heart of the instrument was a flat metal plate drilled with holes corresponding exactly to the positions of the chosen target galaxies in the sky (measured from a photograph). Into these holes were cemented the input-ends of the 20-cm long fibres. The plate was then loaded into the telescope at its focal plane (the place where the image is formed) with the fibres leading off to the spectrograph, spaced back from its normal position immediately behind the telescope's main mirror. When the telescope was pointed accurately towards the selected area of sky, the light from the target galaxies would be picked up by the fibres and delivered securely to the spectrograph slit.

Setting a trend for somewhat whimsical names that seems to have afflicted specialists in astronomical fibre-optics ever since, Hill christened his device 'Medusa' – an apt name, even if the instrument's actual resemblance to the snake-haired Gorgon was less than striking! Medusa was first tried, with 20 fibres, in December 1979, and the galaxy spectra successfully obtained heralded the dawn of the new era of multi-fibre spectroscopy. Amid some scepticism from conservatives in the scientific community, a small revolution in astronomy had begun.

It was not long before other major observatories began planning Medusa-type instruments, with pre-drilled plug-plates to position the fibres. One of the earliest and, for many years, certainly the most productive in terms of data collected about the Universe, was FOCAP, the 'Fibre-Optically Coupled Aperture Plate' system built for the 3.9-metre Anglo-Australian Telescope by Peter Gray of the AAT's engineering staff. (Peter was one of a handful of early specialists who surveyed the world's optical-fibre industry to find fibres suitable for astronomical applications, for many communications-type fibres are not. Fortunately, it transpired that there are one or two specialist manufacturers whose products can be tailored, within limits, to astronomers' requirements.) FOCAP pioneered the use of special plug fittings, or ferrules, on the ends of the fibres, to allow them to be re-used many times with different plug-plates. More than any other system, it showed the versatility of the multi-fibre technique for many different types of astronomical observation and, throughout the 1980s, spectacularly increased the output of the telescope.

Other early converts to the gospel of multi-fibre spectroscopy were the 3.6-metre telescope of the European Southern Observatory in Chile and, in Arizona, the 4-metre telescope of the Kitt Peak National Observatory. Here, plug-plate systems with the curiously fishy names of 'Fibre Optopus' and 'Nessie' were developed and successfully used in astronomical observing programmes.

Help from computers

Even in the earliest days of multi-fibre spectroscopy it was apparent that the plug-plate system of accurately positioning fibres in the telescope was not necessarily the best. While the holes could be drilled with computer-controlled milling machines, reducing the

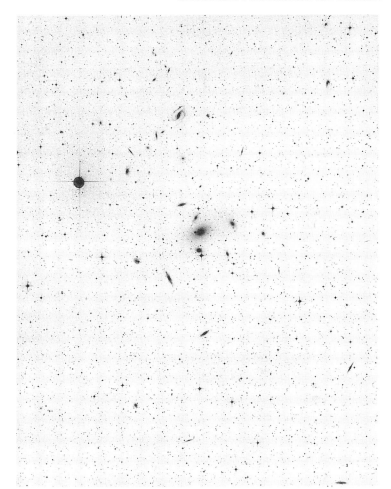

Figure 2. Cluster of galaxies in the southern constellation of Pavo, shown in a portion of a negative obtained with the UK Schmidt Telescope. The first multi-fibre systems, with their limited sky-coverage, were designed to look at concentrated groups of objects. Galaxy clusters like this one provided perfect targets, allowing valuable data on most of the galaxies in the cluster to be collected in a single observation. More recent multi-fibre systems, covering wider fields of view, allow efficient observation of unclustered objects too. (Copyright Royal Observatory, Edinburgh)

possibility of human error, the need to manufacture plug-plates in advance (itself an expensive process) and the need to re-plug a new plate manually when changing from observing one part of the sky to

185

another placed severe limitations on flexibility of observing. Moreover, there was no possibility of slightly changing the position of any of the fibres during observing to 'tweak up' the signal from target stars or galaxies, as might be required when, for example, refraction of light by the Earth's atmosphere produces a mismatch between the images formed by the telescope and the holes drilled in the plate.

It was, again, Angel's group in Arizona that built the first fibre positioner to dispense with a plug-plate. Their 'MX' system (named in parody of a famous cold-war ballistic missile system) used 32 fibres mounted on the tips of computer-actuated rods that could be moved around individually in the focal plane of the telescope. The rods protruded into the focal plane just like the rods of fishermen around a circular pond. Thus, the computer could tell each fibre exactly where to go to intercept the light of a target star or galaxy, and re-configuring the fibres to a new set of targets was simply a question of pressing a button. MX took several years to build, and cost something like a quarter of a million US dollars, but by 1986 it was successfully working on the Steward Observatory 2.3-metre telescope.

The high cost of MX resulted from the need to provide a separate actuator for each fibre – 32 in all. By today's standards, 32 fibres is rather few, but building an MX system for, say, 100 fibres would require impossibly high funding. It was this line of reasoning that led Dr Ian Parry and his colleagues at Durham University, together with Peter Gray, to devise a different computer-controlled technique for positioning fibres – the 'Autofib' system.

Imagine the input end of each fibre fitted with a tiny right-angled prism to deflect the incoming light into it, and then fitted with a magnetic base underneath the prism. Such a 'fibre-button', with its fibre trailing away from it to the spectrograph, could be placed on a steel plate and held there by its own magnetism. Moreover, it could be placed by a computer-controlled robot arm fitted with a mechanical gripper to pick up the button, move it accurately to another part of the steel plate, and put it down again. This is the basis of Autofib – the metal plate lies in the focal plane of the telescope, and as many fibre-buttons as are required by the spectrograph are held there magnetically.

Working under the control of a computer that remembers exactly where each button is, the robot arm can re-arrange the fibre-buttons to any desired configuration matching the target stars and galaxies in the sky. Autofib is what might be called a 'pick/place' device, and its chief advantage over MX is that only one robot is required,

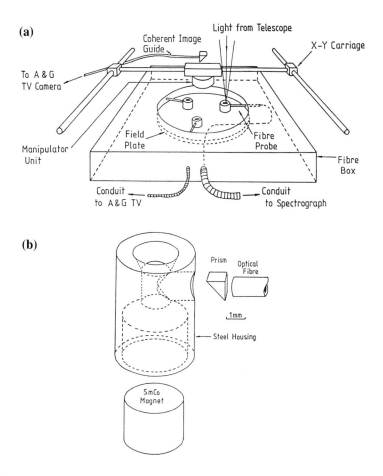

Figure 3. **(a)** *Schematic view of the original Autofib, showing how the fibre probes adhere magnetically to the metal field plate. They are moved accurately from one target position to another by means of the manipulator mounted on the (x, y) carriage. Three of the prismatic 'fibre-buttons' are depicted; the latest version of Autofib (for the Anglo-Australian Telescope's 2dF project) will have more than 400! Some of the acquisition and guidance facilities for aligning the fibres correctly on the sky are also shown.*

(b) *Detail of a fibre-button, showing the miniature prism that directs the telescope beam into the optical fibre. Buttons for the recent versions of Autofib are much more compact. (Courtesy Dr Ian Parry)* saving enormously on cost. The penalty for this is that Autofib takes longer to set up its fibres than MX (which effectively positions them all simultaneously), but high-speed robotics allows the time to be limited to about ten minutes for 100 fibres.

The first Autofib was fitted to the Anglo-Australian Telescope early in 1987, and has been working there ever since. In the same way as MX has spawned a number of imitators, Autofib has become the prototype for a whole class of pick/place fibre positioners built for telescopes in the USA, Europe, and Japan.

Wide-field spectroscopy with flair and panache

In 1982, during the early days of multi-fibre spectroscopy, two astronomers at the 1.2-metre UK Schmidt Telescope in Australia uncovered a simple fact that eventually brought about a radical change in the way the telescope was used. One was Dr John Dawe, then astronomer-in-charge at the telescope, while his collaborator was none other than your humble author.

Our realization that for multi-fibre spectroscopy, the field of view of a telescope and the size of its mirror are of equal importance had particular significance for the Schmidt telescope. At that time, multi-fibre systems were envisaged only for large telescopes with limited fields of view (no more than three-quarters of a degree – about one and a half times the Moon's diameter). The UKST has a modest aperture of only 1.2 metres, but has a field almost 10 degrees across, allowing it to see at any one time a staggering 70 times more sky area than a conventional reflector. Our study showed that a multi-fibre system on the Schmidt could yield an enormous amount of valuable data on brighter stars, galaxies, and quasars. These objects are spread too thinly over the sky to be observed with the larger, small-field telescopes in any other way than one at a time. Thus, for example, with the UKST, 17th magnitude galaxies could be efficiently observed not only in clusters, but spread generally over the sky, allowing major surveys of our local environment in the Universe to be carried out.

The UKST had been designed and built for one purpose only: that of wide-field photography of the southern sky. It fell to yours truly to develop a multi-fibre system that would work efficiently and yet would be interchangeable with the telescope's continuing photographic work. The resulting instrument was called FLAIR (for Fibre-Linked Array-Image Reformatter) and the first prototype was tested in 1985. An improved version, PANACHE

(PANoramic Area Coverage with High Efficiency) was introduced in collaboration with Dr Paddy Oates of Durham University during 1988, and saw four years of useful service on the telescope. Meanwhile, a final version was being built, with support from the UK Science and Engineering Research Council and the Anglo-Australian Observatory, for introduction in 1992. This was originally going to be called FINESSE, until someone pointed out that the name *could* be an acronym for 'Fails to Interest Nearly Everyone Save Spectrograph Engineers' so, in the end, we settled for the safer 'FLAIR II'. It is a pleasure to be able to report that this system is now a highly effective component of the telescope's operation, obtaining spectra for something like 5000 target objects a year, and definitely succeeding in interesting lots of people other than spectrograph engineers! Much of the credit for this is due to the operating staff of the UKST, in particular Dr Quentin Parker, who now has responsibility for the instrument.

The new FLAIR uses a hybrid technique for positioning its fibres in the telescope's focus. Like Autofib, it has fibre-buttons equipped with tiny right-angled prisms, but instead of being stuck magnetically to a metal field plate, they are temporarily cemented on to a thin glass copy of the original Schmidt photograph of the target field. Thus, each fibre can be aligned directly with the actual photographic image of the desired object, making accurate positioning relatively straightforward. This set-up procedure is carried out off the telescope in a positioning laboratory prior to observing, and is assisted by a robot known to its friends as 'AutoFred'. After use, the fibre-buttons can be removed from the plate ready to be set up on the next one.

The instrument offers astronomers various options of fibre numbers and diameters. Up to 92 fibres can be used at any one time, and the maximum available diameter is one-tenth of a millimetre – enough to capture most of the light from the nucleus of a 17th magnitude galaxy. The small size of this dimension gives some idea of the precision needed in positioning the fibres (about one-hundredth of a millimetre).

FLAIR was the world's first wide-field fibre-optic spectroscopy system, but it also pioneered another aspect of the multi-fibre technique now found on several other telescopes. The high transparency and flexibility of the fibres provide an opportunity not only to re-arrange the distribution of the target objects into a neat line for the spectrograph, but also to make the fibres long enough to

Figure 4. The 1.2-metre UK Schmidt Telescope (UKST) was operated until 1988 by the Royal Observatory, Edinburgh, but is now part of the Anglo-Australian Observatory. Experiments with wide-field multi-fibre spectroscopy began in the mid-1980s, and the telescope is seen here with an early version of the FLAIR spectrograph mounted on its laboratory bench in the foreground. Fibre-optic cables bring the light from stars, galaxies, and quasars to the bench. Since 1992, the improved FLAIR II system has allowed detailed spectroscopic observations of up to 92 objects at a time, providing a valuable additional capability to the telescope's normal photographic mode. (Copyright Royal Observatory, Edinburgh)

remove the spectrograph from the telescope altogether and mount it separately in a stationary position. Here it will be immune to the

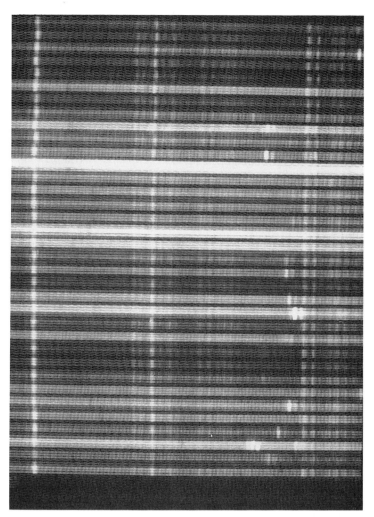

Figure 5. This picture illustrates succinctly why multi-fibre spectroscopy is such an effective survey technique. It shows the spectra of 32 distant galaxies obtained in a single observation with PANACHE – a forerunner of today's FLAIR II – on the UKST. Each horizontal band is the light of a galaxy drawn out into its spectrum colours; the different intensities result from galaxies of different brightness. (Two of the faintest bands are reference spectra of empty sky.) Crossing these in straight lines from top to bottom are bright emission lines that originate high in the Earth's atmosphere, but at the right-hand end are groups of emission lines staggered with respect to one another. These originate in the target galaxies themselves, and have been redshifted along the spectra by amounts proportional to the galaxies' velocities and hence, by the Hubble law, to their distances. Thus, multi-fibre spectroscopy renders direct distance measurements of large numbers of galaxies possible without enormous amounts of telescope time. (Copyright Royal Observatory, Edinburgh: Courtesy Dr Quentin Parker)

tendency to bend under its own weight as it tracks across the sky, and thus will be extremely stable. FLAIR's spectrograph, with its liquid-nitrogen-cooled CCD camera, sits on a laboratory table in the dome, a flexible cable containing the fibres snaking back across the floor to the telescope.

Perhaps more than any other component of FLAIR, this cable encapsulates the effectiveness of the multi-fibre technique, for it carries within it the entire optical output of the telescope – typically the faint light from 90 or so distant galaxies. Standing in the darkened Schmidt dome in the stillness of an Australian night, the telescope humming quietly as it guides automatically on the target field, it is easy to imagine that by picking up the fibre cable in your hand, you would be able to feel those unbelievably ancient photons pulsing through your fingers as they race toward their final destination in the spectrograph camera.

The next generation

The second generation of multi-fibre spectroscopy systems is already with us. The plug-plates of the early 1980s have given way to automated instruments like MX and Autofib that are part of the standard repertoire of the world's great observatories. But we are now on the brink of a new generation of instruments, engineered with a sophistication that would have seemed unbelievable in those early days when fibre-optics spectroscopy was deemed the province of a few loonies on the radical fringe.

For telescopes in the 4-metre class, the emphasis is now on instruments at prime focus (the main focus of the primary mirror) rather than, as hitherto, at Cassegrain (the main focus re-imaged through a hole in the primary by means of a convex secondary mirror). The advantage offered by the prime focus is a wider field of view, though it is still very much less than that of the Schmidt telescope. But, as with FLAIR, the fibre positioning has to be more accurate because of the smaller scale of the image. In order to form a defect-free image at all at prime focus, large telescopes need a system of correcting lenses near the focal plane. Prompted by earlier studies by Professor Charles Wynne (one of the UK's most venerable optical designers), correcting lenses have now been designed that provide wider fields suitable for multi-fibre work.

On the 4.2-metre William Herschel Telescope in La Palma, such a prime-focus corrector with a one-degree field has recently been commissioned. Ian Parry's group at Durham is building a new,

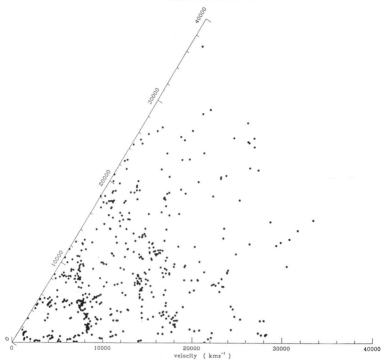

Figure 6. A slice through the local part of the Universe, centred on the Earth, showing the positions of several hundred galaxies. This map, or cone diagram, has been drawn using galaxy distances provided by FLAIR spectra similar to those in Figure 5. The distance scale is shown as a velocity (or redshift); very roughly, 30,000 kms⁻¹ corresponds to 1000 million light-years. The map shows that the distribution of galaxies is not uniform on these very large scales. (Courtesy Dr Alison Broadbent)

smarter Autofib ('AF-2') that will feed 150 fibres from the prime focus to an instrument known as WYFFOS (WYde-Field Fibre-Optics Spectrograph!) being built by the Royal Greenwich Observatory, Cambridge. WYFFOS will sit, not on the dome floor, but in an enclosure on the telescope's 'Nasmyth platform'. This moves around with the telescope mounting, but always remains horizontal and is thus inherently stable.

To reach down to WYFFOS, the fibres must be 26 metres long and, so that AF-2 can be removed from the telescope without removing the fibre cables too, they include connectors that allow each fibre to be broken into two halves. This straightforward-sounding operation is very difficult to achieve without seriously

Figure 7. An unusual view of the 4.2-metre William Herschel Telescope, taken from beneath the telescope mounting. To the left and right of the telescope's centre section are the two Nasmyth platforms (with light-coloured handrails), which remain horizontal no matter where the telescope is pointing. One of these now boasts an enclosed cabin for high-resolution imaging; this will also be the home of WYFFOS, the WHT's new multi-fibre spectrograph. It will be fed by fibres from the Autofib-2 robotic positioner at prime focus (in the centre of the top-end ring). (Copyright Royal Greenwich Observatory)

degrading the performance of the re-joined fibres, and considerable development work has been carried out at the RGO and Durham University. Similar connectors might well feature on future large-telescope fibre-optics systems.

Down-under in New South Wales, substantial resources have been invested in a prime-focus corrector system for the Anglo-Australian Telescope with a two-degree field – the '2dF' project initiated by Dr Keith Taylor and Peter Gray. The four square-degrees of sky coverage will be the biggest of any 4-metre class telescope in the world, and will provide a major tool for survey spectroscopy of southern stars, galaxies, and quasars that are too faint for FLAIR.

The fibre positioner will be an Autofib system, with a refinement that allows *two* interchangeable field plates to be patrolled by the positioning robot. While the fibres on one field plate are collecting light from the target objects, those on the other are being re-configured for the next field. 2dF will feed no less than 400 fibres simultaneously to two spectrographs mounted near the prime focus at the top of the telescope. (The reason they will not be placed down on the dome floor is to keep the fibres short, for there is a trade-off between the length of a fibre and its transmission of ultraviolet and blue light. 2dF is thus being optimized for blue transmission at the cost of some stability.) A high degree of sophistication is needed in the computer programs used to keep track of all those fibres – not to mention the software designed to analyse the copious quantities of data that 2dF will produce.

By the time these words appear in print, both WYFFOS and 2dF will be starting work on their respective telescopes. Another new development has a less predictable future. The arrival in the last few years of TV-type detectors sensitive to infrared (heat) radiation has prompted the introduction of a new generation of astronomical infrared spectrographs that might be adaptable to multi-fibre work. The problem in the so-called 'thermal infrared' is that *everything*, including the sky, the telescope and its auxiliary equipment, radiates far more heat than the target objects. Moreover, ordinary fused-silica fibres do not work in this region of the electromagnetic spectrum, and the specialized fibres needed are expensive and fragile. On top of all this, telescopes designed for infrared observations usually have such small fields of view that the advantages of multi-fibre observing are limited.

Nevertheless, a collaboration exists between the University of Durham and the two Royal Observatories (Edinburgh and Cambridge) to explore the possibility of using fibres on UKIRT, the 3.8-metre UK Infra-Red Telescope in Hawaii. The successful implementation of fibre-optics for infrared spectroscopy is, overall, an attractive prospect, and is being pursued by a number of groups throughout the world. It represents, perhaps, the next major step in the continuing fibre-optics revolution.

Beyond these developments are the prospects of completely new telescopes equipped with multi-fibre systems. Plans exist for a number of large instruments in the USA with dedicated multi-object spectroscopy facilities for specialized surveys of the sky. At least one of these (the Sloan Digital Sky Survey telescope) will eschew automation and use a refined version of the plug-plate method. But for most people, perhaps, interest is focused on the giant 8-metre class telescopes that are now materializing: the two 10-metre Keck telescopes, the Japanese *Subaru* 8-metre, the 4 × 8-metre European Southern Observatory Very Large Telescope and, of especial interest to astronomers in Britain, the two Gemini 8-metre telescopes, in which we have a 25 per cent share. For Gemini at least, a multi-fibre capability is planned, although it does not at present have a high priority. As with most of these giant instruments, the present thrust is towards active image-sharpening to overcome atmospheric turbulence and bring about high-resolution imaging of very faint objects.

Epilogue – a personal view . . .

I should like to end this article where it began, with the excitement of a simple, effective new technique being brought to astronomy by virtue of a new product (low-loss optical fibres) and lots of creative thinking by the likes of Angel, Hill, and Gray. Having been privileged to work in the field of astronomical fibre-optics since the very early days, I have seen all kinds of possibilities explored and clever ideas evolved, and generally watched with enthusiasm the progress of the 'multi-fibre revolution'. I often wonder what will be the next simple idea that will change the way we do astronomy. What new spin-off from our technological society will provide another Roger Angel with a novel tool that will be taken up enthusiastically by the scientific community?

For what it's worth, I'll give you my tip for the fibre-optics business. I predict that infrared fibres will become a hot topic (forgive the pun) and will be followed by a new trend in spectrograph design. Multi-object spectrographs will be miniaturized and will use the guided-light principles that allow fibres themselves to work, rather than conventional optical components. It will be possible to immerse the spectrograph entirely in a liquid-helium bath to reduce background heat-noise, and provide very efficient multi-object spectroscopy of faint infrared sources ranging from young stars in dust clouds to the most distant galaxies.

Exciting stuff? So far, it's only a hunch. But remember where you heard it first!

Minor Bodies in the Outer Solar System

IWAN P. WILLIAMS

Introduction

By a strange twist of fate, the Minor Planet story started on the first day of the nineteenth century, that is on January 1, 1801, when an object was discovered by Piazzi at Palermo. This discovery was not a serendipitous discovery, but the culmination of a long search. In 1766, Johann Titius had pointed out in a footnote in a book that the distances of the then known six planets seemed to follow a simple mathematical progression, a fact which was also noted by Johann Elert Bode in 1772. When Herschel discovered the planet Uranus in 1781, it was immediately evident that Uranus fitted into the progression remarkably well. The same progression indicated that there should be a planet orbiting between Mars and Jupiter, hence the search. However, astronomers soon realized that the object, now named Ceres, was much too faint to be the hoped-for planet. The situation became more confused with the discovery by Olbers of a second body, Pallas, in the gap on March 28, 1802, and two more, Juno by Harding on September 1, 1804 and Vesta, again by Olbers, on March 29, 1807. The term 'Minor Planets', which is still the official International Astronomical Union terminology, was invented for these objects. William Herschel wanted a more up-beat name and coined the name 'asteroids' a name that seems to be more popular.

The total number of asteroids known remained constant at four for nearly forty years. This came to an end when Hencke discovered Astræa on December 8, 1845. Since that date there have been very regular new discoveries, with over 5000 known by now. The vast majority are located between the orbits of Mars and Jupiter. However, a number can be found in other regions. There is a set which can approach or even cross the orbit of the Earth. These strictly consist of three groups, the Apollo, Amor, and Aten, named after the first asteroid of each group to be found. The differences between these three groups are rather technical and indeed it is quite conceivable that an individual asteroid can switch from one group to the other. Taken together, they form a set that has aroused considerable interest in the popular press of late through the possibility of one of them colliding with the Earth. There is also a group of a few hundred asteroids, the Trojan asteroids, that move on orbits very similar to that of Jupiter, their motion being one of librating around the Lagrangian equilibrium points, 60° either side of the location of Jupiter. However, for a long time, the volume beyond Jupiter had been considered to be the domain of the comets, that is bodies that moved on highly eccentric orbits, spending most of their time in the outer reaches of the Solar System but making the occasional excursion into the inner system where they produced the well-known and occasionally spectacular tails. It is to this region that we want to focus our attention.

Asteroids beyond Jupiter

The first asteroid to be discovered moving on an orbit that took it truly beyond Jupiter was 944 Hidalgo, discovered in 1920 by Baade. Hidalgo moves on a fairly elliptical orbit with an eccentricity of 0.66. Its mean distance from the Sun is 5.8 AU and the orbit is very similar to that of comet Wild I (1973 VIII). Even with its elliptical orbit, it does not quite reach the orbit of Saturn and for a long time it was regarded as an abnormal asteroid, ejected on to such an orbit by effects such as collisions and gravitational perturbations, from the main belt. Such an explanation may well be true for Hidalgo, and so the astronomical community was able to preserve the notion that asteroids were confined to a belt between Mars and Jupiter but with perturbations and collisions affecting a small number so that they are now seen slightly outside the belt. Comets on the other hand originated at great distances from the Sun in the Oort cloud, named after Jan Oort who postulated its existence in 1950 from a study of the orbits of long-period comets. Those that got perturbed into the planetary region would have high eccentricity. The first dramatic discovery that would change this came in 1977 when Charles Kowal discovered 2060 Chiron. It spends almost all its time orbiting between Saturn and Uranus, with a mean distance of 13.7 AU. Though the orbit is significantly elliptical with an eccentricity of 0.38, this is within the range found for 'normal' asteroids and is significantly smaller than most comets. At first this was hailed as the discovery of the tenth planet, a story to be repeated fifteen years later, but, as with the original discovery of Ceres, it was soon realized that Chiron is far too small to be regarded as a planet, being no more than 100 km across, a decent asteroid but hardly a planet. As is often the case in Solar System studies, nothing of real significance occurred for over ten years, almost until the 90s when a number of important discoveries took place. Six years ago, Chiron increased in brightness by about a magnitude as it approached perihelion inside the orbit of Saturn. The explanation for this became apparent when Karen Meech and Mike Belton detected a coma about Chiron. The existence of the coma was subsequently verified by a number of other observers including the author. Whether the coma formed by genuine outgassing (i.e. driven by sublimation of ices due to Solar heating) or by some other cause such as the one which generated a similar brightening and formation of a dust envelope around comet Halley when at about the same heliocentric distance in 1989 is a moot point, but it does suggest that Chiron is a quasi-dormant comet that has been mis-identified as an asteroid. In 1991, a second asteroid, 1991 DA, was discovered moving in the same general region as Chiron. It has a more elongated orbit with an eccentric of 0.87 and so at various times crosses the orbits of Jupiter, Saturn, and Uranus. Its orbit is thus very comet-like, but no coma has been discovered about it. In 1992 a third object of this class, 5145 Pholus (1992 DA) was discovered. As its mean heliocentric distance is 20.4 AU it spends most of its life just outside the orbit of Uranus, but its orbit can cross both those of Saturn and Neptune. These three are sometimes described as the Centaur group. Numerical integration shows that these orbits are unstable on time scales shorter than the age of the Solar System, indicating that these objects have been captured on to such orbits from some other location almost certainly outside the planetary region. These three distant asteroids are thus almost certainly dormant or semi-dormant comets, and highlight the problem facing astronomers in deciding what is an asteroid and what is a comet when the object concerned is abnormal in some way.

As already mentioned, comets have generally been assumed to originate from the Oort cloud. Today, the 'Oort cloud' is an accepted part of our Solar System, containing perhaps 10^{12} comets at distances of up to 50,000 AU from the Sun, though none has actually been detected. Just a year later, Gerard Kuiper hypothesized that there might be a second comet cloud much nearer than the Oort cloud. At distances greater than 30–40 AU, the space density of proto-planetary material would be too low to support

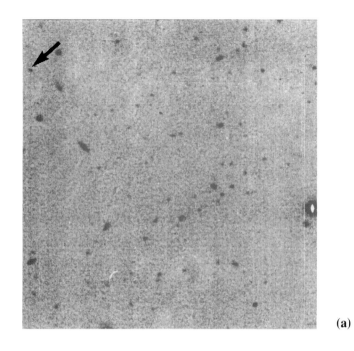

(a)

(b)

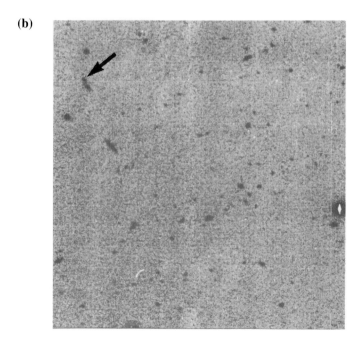

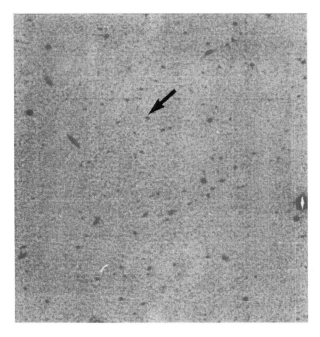

(c)

Figure 1. Three IRAF images of 1993SC. (**a**) *Run 208 on Sept. 17, 1993:* (**b**) *Run 217 on same date: and* (**c**) *Run 308.*
The time interval between 208 and 217 is about 4½ hours, with 19 hours between 217 and 308. Between 208 and 308 the motion was −5.32 seconds of time in RA and −32.8″ in declination. Arrows indicate 1993 SC.

continued accretion of bodies greater in size than a few hundred kilometres across. However, it is unlikely that formation of bodies in the Solar System ceased sharply with the planets in a solar nebula model, but rather continued more and more inefficiently as the time for growth became longer and longer. This would result in smaller icy bodies being found further away. Indeed one can claim to see evidence of this with the smaller ice bodies of Pluto, its moon Charon, and Triton, the large retrograde moon of Neptune which is obviously a captured moon, being the next size down from Uranus and Neptune. Smaller bodies would also naturally form with increasing distance. Interest in this possible 'Kuiper Belt' of comets remained cautious or even non-existent until the late 1980s when studies of the orbital evolution of comets coming from the Oort cloud and undergoing planetary perturbations could not reproduce the observed distribution of orbital inclinations of short-period comets in the inner Solar System. This problem was heightened with the discovery of the Centaur group of asteroids mentioned above. In particular, the mean orbital inclination of the short period comets is only 10 degrees, which cannot be created from an initial isotropic distribution of Oort cloud comets. This problem could be overcome only if the short period comets had a source in a disk of comets lying in the general plane of the Solar System. Hence an observational need for a Kuiper belt arose. Unfortunately, a need does not prove the existence, and until Kuiper belt objects are found, they remain as nothing but a theory.

The search beyond Neptune

Unfortunately Kuiper belt objects would be extremely faint due to both their large heliocentric distance and probable dark colour, implying a low visual albedo of only about 4 per cent. Nevertheless several searches took place between 1989 and 1992 using both photographic and CCD techniques. All were unsuccessful, and the general consensus was that Kuiper belt objects brighter than about 22 magnitude did not exist. However, CCD technology developed so that it was possible to take deeper images and so detect fainter objects, and finally a long search by David Jewitt and Jane Luu was rewarded when a very slow-moving faint object was detected in September 1992 and given the temporary designation 1992 QB1. From images obtained three and a half weeks apart it was deduced that one possible orbit was almost circular at a distance of about 42 AU, just beyond the orbit of Pluto. Subsequent observations of 1992 QB1 have confirmed that the orbit is nearly circular, and so 1992 QB1 became a good candidate for a Kuiper belt object. However, one object hardly constitutes a belt, and so the search continued for other bodies. Six months later, in March 1993, Jewitt and Luu found a second slow-moving object, 1993 FW. At this time Alan Fitzsimmons and Donal O'Ceallaigh from Queen's University Belfast and the author also joined the search.

The 2.5-metre Isaac Newton Telescope at the Roque de los Muchachos Observatory on La Palma in the Canaries with a CCD camera at the prime focus and the large format Ford-Loral CCD chip provide an excellent piece of instrumentation with which to search for faint slow-moving objects. The pixel size of 0.37 arcsec allows adequate sampling even during sub-arcsecond seeing, while the large area of 12.6 arcminutes square enhances the probability of detection. The technique is simply to obtain two images separated by a period of around three hours in time, and inspect them for moving objects. All objects moving on a near circular orbit at distances in excess of 30 AU appear to retrograde slowly along the ecliptic at rates of under 4 arcsec per hour, most of the apparent motion arising from the movement of the Earth. At such a rate a motion of about 30 pixels is obtained in three hours, easily detectable but unlikely to take the object outside the field of view. Any objects detected are then imaged again on the following days so that some orbital information can be obtained. This mode of working has the unfortunate side effect that all the images obtained on the first night must be fully analysed before starting to observe on the second night, so that both sleeping and admiring the scenery become very hard.

In September 1993 we had one week of time on the Isaac Newton Telescope with the above-mentioned instrumentation and obtained deep R-band images. We believed that any existing Kuiper belt objects would be found close to the ecliptic while their apparent motion would be greater if measured near opposition. These two considerations define the position around RA 23 hours 52 minutes, declination −0 degrees 30 minutes and in the time available we imaged 0.5 square degrees of sky. In clear weather and good seeing, 30 minute exposures allowed us to achieve a magnitude limit of ~24 in R. However, the limiting magnitude was highly sensitive to seeing and that our effective limiting magnitude for the entire run was probably around 22.5 magnitude.

As these things go, we found one slow-moving object within a few hours of starting work and a second on the following night. However, the remaining five nights yielded no further objects. These have been given the temporary designations of 1993 SB and 1993 SC. 1993 SB was barely visible at R = 22.7, while 1993 SC was much easier to detect at R = 21.7. Assuming near circular orbits, they are at distances of 33.1 AU and 34.5 AU respectively. They are thus much nearer the Sun than the two objects found by Jewitt and Luu, and are between Neptune and Pluto. At essentially the same time, Jewitt and Luu discovered two more objects, 1993 RO and 1993 RP, also between Neptune and Pluto. The known data on these six objects are given in Table 1. Thus, if these are Kuiper belt objects, then the belt starts much closer to the Sun than had hitherto been imagined and makes Pluto into a very Kuiper belt object rather than a true planet. In this event the possibility of there being any further planets beyond Pluto yet to be discovered is slim in the extreme. However, a quirk of the timing of the observations in

September 1993 means that the search area was about 60° away from Neptune along its orbit. This is, of course, the position of one of the Lagrangian equilibrium points around which Trojans librate. Thus it is possible that these four objects are Trojans of Neptune rather than Kuiper belt objects.

Brian Marsden has recently pointed out that orbits similar to Pluto's, that is on a 3:2 resonance with Neptune, are also consistent with the data.

Whatever the truth, it is certain that the outer Solar System is a far more exciting place than we would have imagined a few years ago, and that many further observations are necessary before we will reach the truth.

TABLE 1

Object	Semi-Major Axis (AU)	Diameter (km)
Saturn	9.6	120660
1991 DA	11.9	
2060 Chiron	13.7	<300
Halley's Comet	17.9	16
Uranus	19.2	52400
5145 Pholus	20.4	
Comet Swift–Tuttle	26.3	
Neptune	30.1	50460
1993 RO	32.3:	150
1993 SB	33.1:	150
1993 SC	34.5:	300
1993 RP	35.4:	100
Pluto	39.4	2400
1992 QB1	43.8	200
1993 FW	43.9	150

The Early Volcanic History of Some Asteroids

LIONEL WILSON

Everyone agrees that the asteroids, those minor planetary bodies with orbits lying mainly between those of Mars and Jupiter, hold some of the most important clues to the origin and early history of the Solar System. This is because some of the asteroids do not seem to have evolved significantly since the time they were formed. From Earth, these bodies have mainly been studied spectroscopically, by measuring the intensity and polarization of the sunlight reflected off them over a wide range of wavelengths. Various common minerals can be identified by the way they absorb light at particular infrared wavelengths, and so these studies have allowed several major classes of asteroid to be identified which have surface chemical compositions similar to those of well-known types of meteorite. This is not surprising, since the great majority of meteorites are likely to be fragments broken off the surfaces of asteroids or comets in high-speed collisions.

So far, the only space-craft to fly close to any true asteroids has been Galileo, which has made close approaches to 951 Gaspra in 1991 and 243 Ida in 1993. However, since almost everyone agrees that the small satellites of Mars, Phobos, and Deimos can be regarded as asteroids, we should also include the Mariner 9 and Viking Orbiter images of these two bodies. The images of all four objects show them to have irregular body shapes, extensively pock-marked with impact craters, consistent with the origins of meteorites. Infrared scans of Phobos by the Soviet space-craft Phobos-2 suggest a surface composition similar to that of the C-type main-belt asteroids, apparently closely related to the carbonaceous chondrite meteorites, whereas 243 Ida is known from Earth-based measurements to have a surface composition similar to that of stony meteorites. There are other significant differences between the four bodies: Deimos seems to have a thicker layer of impact-derived fragmental rock on its surface than the others (these layers are called 'regoliths'), while both 243 Ida and 951 Gaspra have larger numbers of small craters than either of the Martian moons. Phobos has three groups of linear or gently curving depressions (called 'grooves') on its surface. Some of these grooves may have been formed by the rolling and bouncing of blocks of rock thrown out of the largest crater on Phobos, called Stickney; others seem to show evidence of drainage of the surface regolith into fractures extending deeply through the body; and others have the right orientations to have been caused by fragments ejected from impact craters on the surface of Mars itself. Some images of 951 Gaspra also show surface depressions which appear to be grooves of some kind, probably related to internal fractures.

Important though the above data are, close approaches by space-craft can never be certain of allowing us to discover the internal compositions of asteroids. This is because the regolith is produced by generations of large and small impacts on the surface, and so is a complex mixture of rocks from a wide range of depths below the surface of the body. Additionally, bombardment of the outer few microns of the surface rocks by solar radiation (sunlight and atomic particles) alters the physical and chemical properties in complex ways. So until we have space-craft missions which actually rendezvous with asteroids, drill holes into their interiors, and either bring samples back to Earth or make elaborate measurements of the samples on the spot, we will always be in need of the meteorites: our free samples from inside asteroids. The drawback, of course, is that, even when a meteorite is found as a result of its bright fireball path being tracked through the atmosphere photographically, so that the orbit round the Sun can be deduced, we still cannot be sure which asteroid it has come from, and how far below the surface it was located before its removal.

It is partly for this reason that so much effort has been expended over the last few decades in trying to classify the major groups of meteorites in terms of their chemical and physical properties. Their bulk compositions have been determined, their ages (both the time since the last major heating event and the time since the last major impact which, presumably, detached the meteorite from its parent body) have been analysed, and their petrological properties (types and sizes of the mineral grains present) have been measured. Furthermore, these measurements have become very accurate and sensitive: it is now possible to carry out chemical analyses on extremely small amounts of material. This means, for example, that compositional variations across a single small mineral grain can be traced. Taken together, these studies have made it possible to define families of meteorites, not only on the basis of their bulk properties, but also in terms of the often very complex evolutionary processes that they have undergone.

The reasons for the existence of the various meteorite groups which have been detected by the above studies are not always obvious. Some groupings clearly represent the consequences of differing initial compositions, reflecting the accretion of the parent asteroids at differing distances from the proto-Sun, but others can only be understood by thinking through some of the physical processes which must have taken place inside the asteroids. For example, many groups of meteorites have what are called primitive compositions: they contain chemical compounds which are not stable at high temperatures and pressures. This is taken to mean that they can never have been present inside large asteroids (the larger the body the greater the value of the acceleration due to gravity within it and hence the greater the internal pressure), or inside asteroids that got very hot. Other groups of meteorites consist only of minerals that are formed when a rock cools down from a molten state at a high pressure, so they must have formed inside large asteroids, and those asteroids must have been heated in some way. An asteroid may have become hot either by accreting near the Sun, so that it formed from hot materials, or by having an internal heat source. The latter could be the rapid decay of naturally radioactive elements with short half-lives, or the heating produced by electric currents induced when the asteroid was forced to move through the intense magnetic field of the early Sun.

It is clear that some – perhaps many – asteroids did undergo very significant heating, since about 15 per cent of all meteorites are composed mainly of metals, actually iron-nickel alloys rich in sulphur and other elements, which are very similar in composition to the materials which almost certainly form the core of the Earth. Of course, we cannot get samples of the core from inside the Earth, but we can deduce its properties from its density and the speeds of seismic (earthquake) waves passing through it. We also find meteorites composed of the minerals which are common in the Earth's mantle, of which we do have samples occasionally brought to the surface by volcanic eruptions. This degree of chemical and physical differentiation of the interior of a body can only occur if much of its interior melts.

However, the differences between various meteorite groups

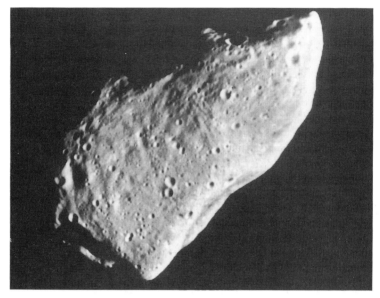

Figure 1. The asteroid 951 Gaspra imaged by the Galileo space-craft en route to Jupiter in 1991. Gaspra measures about 19 × 12 × 11 km.

cannot be understood only in terms of the internal chemical re-arrangements caused by this melting; it is necessary to analyse the physical processes taking place too. A good illustration concerns the group of meteorites called the aubrites, which are stony objects rich in the minerals enstatite and pyroxene. Their trace element chemistry shows that these rocks were formed inside an asteroid which started life with a composition similar to that of the relatively primitive meteorites called enstatite chondrites. A heating event took place inside this body and a basaltic melt, a liquid rich in the elements which form the mineral plagioclase, was formed. Basaltic melts, or just basalts, are the commonest types of volcanic rocks to be erupted now on the surface of the Earth (mainly from long chains of volcanic ridges on the ocean floors). Rocks with very similar compositions were collected by the Apollo astronauts from ancient eruptions in the mare basins on the Moon, and chemical analyses of the surfaces of Venus (by several Soviet Venera and Vega landing probes) and Mars (by the two Viking landers) are also consistent with the presence of the same rock types.

Figure 2. A Galileo image of the 52-km long asteroid 243 Ida.

Inside the enstatite chondrite asteroid, such a basaltic melt would have been lighter than the solids from which it was derived and, as it separated from its surroundings, would have migrated upwards towards the surface under the action of gravity. The residue left behind eventually cooled, and it is this material which has been brought to us, after many impact events had fragmented the parent body, as the aubrite meteorites. Since the impact events have exposed the deep interior of the parent asteroid they should certainly have broken up the outer layers of the body, where the basaltic melts came to rest and solidified. And about the same volume of basaltic rocks should have been formed and subsequently excavated as the volume of the aubrites they left behind. Yet not a single meteorite has ever been found with the right mineralogy and trace element chemistry to represent a sample of this basaltic material. How can this be? Either the above scenario is completely wrong, or the basalts have mysteriously disappeared.

The key to solving the impasse came from applying what we know about volcanic activity on planets like the Earth and Mars. Partial melting of rocks at various depths in the mantle and the subsequent migration of the melts produced towards the surface is the source of all volcanic processes on these bodies. As melts rise from the hot interior into the cooler, more brittle outer layers, they travel inside long, thin cracks, generally called dykes. The gravitational weight of all the overlying rocks causes a pressure in the crack walls which tries to squeeze any such crack closed. But the cracks manage to hold themselves open because the liquid inside them is at a higher pressure than the rocks outside. This internal excess pressure exists because the liquid formed in the melting process is normally less dense than, and so has a larger volume than, the solids from which it is derived; thus, as the liquid forms, an extra pressure must arise to squeeze it into the space originally available for it. As a moving dyke migrates, the interplay between all these pressures causes the rocks ahead of the upper tip of the dyke to crack open, and the rocks behind it to pinch shut again.

The behaviour of molten rock approaching the surface in a crack or dyke depends on how much gas it contains. On the Earth and the other large planets, these gases come from volatile chemical compounds held in solution in the mantle rocks. The volatiles can only remain dissolved at the high pressures found in the deep interiors and so, as the melt nears the surface where the pressure is low, compounds like carbon dioxide, sulphur dioxide, and water exsolve to form gas bubbles. As the pressure decreases, existing gas bubbles get larger and new small bubbles continue to form and grow. If there is enough gas, or if the final pressure is low enough (as it certainly is on small bodies like Mars, where the pressure of the atmosphere is more than one hundred times smaller than on Earth, or the Moon, where there is no atmosphere at all), the volume of the gas bubbles becomes very large. From studies on volcanic rocks we know that, when the gas bubbles occupy more than about 75 to 80 per cent of the total volume, the rock foam disintegrates into a large number of liquid droplets which, by this stage, are being swept up to the surface by the expansion of the gas which is released from between them as the bubbles burst.

We are very familiar with the result of this process on Earth: it is what we call explosive volcanic activity. The ejected droplets and clots of molten rock cool as they are propelled into the atmosphere and they either fall back near the volcanic vent if they are relatively large, or, if they are very small, are carried up into an eruption cloud as their heat warms the surrounding atmosphere with which they mix. Eventually these small particles are deposited some distance away as the cloud cools again. The speed reached by the molten fragments emerging from the vent is relatively high if a large amount of gas is released from the molten rock and also if a lot of gas expansion takes place, i.e. the atmospheric pressure is low. The distance travelled by the fragments depends on three things: how fast they are launched, how much frictional drag the atmosphere exerts on them (a lot if they are very small or the atmosphere is dense, i.e. the pressure is high), and the gravity; they travel further on a planet with low gravity, of course.

How do these factors combine when we think of eruptions on asteroids? All the asteroids are much smaller than the Moon and have never had any appreciable atmosphere. This means that gas expansion during explosive eruptions would have been very effective at producing the highest possible eruption speeds, and that no drag forces slowed down the molten fragments emerging from volcanic vents, even though these droplets would have been very small (generally much less than one millimetre to judge by the ones formed in ancient eruptions on the Moon and found in lunar samples returned by the Apollo missions). Also, the small sizes of the asteroids means that they have low gravity and so the erupted fragments would travel for great distances from the vent. However, there is another aspect of the gravity that is critical to the present story. If a planet has a low gravity it also has a low value for its escape velocity, the minimum speed at which something must be thrown away from the planet to escape completely from its gravitational attraction. Now, planetary scientists had always dismissed the idea that volcanic explosions could throw fragments of rock off planets like the Earth, Mars and the Moon because quite simple calculations show that the amounts of gas needed to launch fragments at the required speeds are vastly greater than the amounts ever observed to exist in volcanic rocks. But, when my colleague at the University of Hawaii, Professor Klaus Keil, and I did the same calculations for the asteroids in 1990, we realized that escape speed could be reached on these bodies in explosive eruptions of melts with much smaller gas contents.

The critical issue was, obviously, just how much gas did the parent asteroid of the aubrite meteorites contain? In 1991, Professor David Muenow, also at the University of Hawaii, made laboratory measurements on pieces of enstatite chondrite meteorites, the primitive rocks that, according to the chemical arguments, apparently formed the aubrite parent body, and showed that they contain quite large amounts (up to several tenths of a per cent by weight) of gas, mainly carbon monoxide and nitrogen, much of it trapped in the spaces between mineral grains. This gas would have been readily available to drive explosive eruptions of the basaltic liquids produced during a melting event on the asteroid, and calculations show that it is enough to have caused the volcanic droplets to reach escape velocity on any parent body up to about 200 km in diameter. The fate of these fragments, once they have escaped from the asteroid, is to go into their own orbits around the Sun. Small objects in such orbits do not last long compared with the 4600-million-year age of the Solar System: the absorption and re-radiation of sunlight exerts a tiny force on them which causes the orbital radius to decrease until eventually the object falls into the Sun (this process is called the Poynting–Robertson effect). For objects much smaller than a millimetre this would take at most a few hundred million years, and thus it is no surprise that we see no sign of the aubrite parent body's basaltic rocks today.

The above work implies that, as long as a small asteroid contains even a small amount of gas, it will find it very hard to retain, on its surface, the erupted basaltic rocks which are the lower density products of partial melting events. Yet some asteroidal basalts do exist, in the form of the eucrite meteorites. Spectroscopic reflectance measurements show that these meteorites almost certainly come from the surface of the asteroid 4 Vesta. The diameter of 4 Vesta is about 560 km, and our calculations show that a gas content of at least 3.5 weight per cent (more than 10 times greater than is common in primitive meteorites) would be needed to blast basaltic droplets off such a body. But the chemistry of the eucrites suggests that they are derived from an unusually volatile-poor parent body. Thus 4 Vesta, as a fairly large and volatile-poor asteroid, is just the kind of body that should have been able to retain its basalts. Bodies like 4 Vesta, perhaps a little smaller so that more of their interiors have been exposed by the impacts that have progressively torn them apart over Solar System history, are ideal targets for future space missions to rendezvous with asteroids.

The most recent work on the physics of melting events on asteroids seems to have found another instance of the important role of gases trapped in these primitive bodies. The story this time begins with the metallic nickel-iron meteorites. On the basis of patterns in the amounts of the minor elements which they contain, the nickel-iron meteorites fall into 13 families, 11 of which have chemistries consistent with the idea mentioned above that they are pieces of the metal cores of 11 different asteroids, each of which underwent very thorough internal differentiation (probably as a result of almost complete melting). The metal in these meteorites exists in a crystalline form, and the sizes of the crystals show how fast the cores cooled after the melting was over and so how large the parent body was: a large body loses heat more slowly and the slower cooling causes the growth of larger crystals. Now the nickel-iron meteorites contain significant amounts of the element sulphur, and the quantities of sulphur in the meteorites also correlate with the parent body size; meteorites from the largest bodies (estimated to have been at least 150 km in diameter) generally contain a little more than 10 per cent sulphur, roughly the same as the H-type chondrite meteorites, judged to be unaltered samples of the primitive material from which the differentiated asteroids formed. Meteorites from smaller parent bodies contain less sulphur, ranging down to less than 1 per cent for samples from parents about 50 km in diameter. Thus the smaller asteroids somehow lost up to 90 per cent of their initial sulphur during their melting episodes.

Although various proposals had been made to explain this loss, none of them was very plausible in terms of the physical mechanisms involved. Last year, Klaus Keil and I looked at this problem again and formulated the following explanation. We know from arguments based on thermodynamics that, if any melting had started in an asteroid with H-type chondrite composition, the first melt to form would have been an iron-nickel sulphide liquid, a compound of iron, nickel, and sulphur. Although it would have been rich in the light element sulphur, the melt would have been denser than the surrounding rocks from which it was separating, so that it should have tried to migrate downwards to start to form a central core. Later in the heating event, as the temperature got higher, it would have been joined by a more nearly pure iron liquid to form a core with about 10 per cent sulphur, as is observed in the coarsely crystalline meteorite samples.

However, we know on the basis of laboratory measurements that the H-chondrite rocks, like the enstatite chondrites, should have contained about a tenth of a weight per cent of gases such as nitrogen and carbon monoxide. When we worked out the combined density, at the pressures inside asteroids of various sizes, of an iron-nickel sulphide liquid containing the appropriate amount of gas bubbles, we found that it was less dense than the surrounding rocks, so that the mixture should in fact have tried to rise to the surface! If about 90 per cent of this sulphide liquid had been expelled at a speed higher than the escape velocity in a series of explosive volcanic eruptions, like the ones on the aubrite parent body discussed above, we would have a perfect explanation for the sulphur depleted asteroid cores represented by the fine-grained meteorites. But clearly not all the asteroids lost nearly all of the sulphide liquid: for some reason the liquid was retained more efficiently on the larger asteroids. Why should this be?

The answer lies in following the fate of the gas bubbles distributed throughout the sulphide liquid. The gas bubbles were much less dense than the liquid – sufficiently so that the bulk density of the mixture was less than that of the rest of the asteroid. So while the liquid with its entrained gas bubbles was tunnelling its way towards the surface by opening cracks in the surrounding rocks, at the same time the gas bubbles were drifting upwards through the liquid. If it ever happened that most of the gas in a crack managed to collect at the top end of the crack, the pressures exerted on the walls and tips of the crack would have changed dramatically. The walls would have pinched together, not only at the bottom of the crack in the normal way, but also at a point near the boundary between the gas-filled upper part and the liquid-filled lower part, thus separating the original crack into two. The new upper crack, filled almost entirely with very buoyant gas, would carry on rising to the surface to discharge its gas into space. The new lower crack would now contain only dense sulphide liquid and would reverse its direction, attempting to fracture its way back down to the centre of the asteroid!

Clearly the critical issue concerns the relative values of the speed at which gas bubbles can rise through the sulphide melt and the speed at which melt-filled cracks can propagate. Both these speeds depend on the viscosity of the sulphide liquid and on the value of the gravity inside the asteroid, which is in turn a function of its size and the depth of the crack. Quite complex calculations are needed to work out these two speeds, especially as other processes may be going on which have not been mentioned so far: larger cracks can overtake and join together with smaller ones, for example, and large bubbles can absorb smaller ones if they catch up with them. Nevertheless these calculations can be done, even if only approximately in some cases. They show that, in small asteroids, the gas should not have segregated very efficiently to the tops of rising cracks, so that most of the sulphide liquid should have been erupted at the surface. In large asteroids the reverse is true: as cracks neared the surface, the gas would have escaped, leaving the liquid to descend again to the core. This is just the pattern actually seen, of course. What is more, the calculations show that the change in behaviour should occur at an asteroid size of roughly 150 km, again consistent with the asteroid sizes deduced from the size of the nickel-iron crystals.

Finally, it must be said that there are still many things that we do not understand in connection with the melting of asteroids (in addition to the issue of just exactly where the heat came from!). Earlier I talked about the basalts and the aubrites on the aubrite parent asteroid, but I did not consider the whereabouts of the iron-nickel sulphide liquid that should have formed somewhere inside that body early in the melting process. And though I mentioned the early-forming sulphide liquid, and the later, nearly pure iron liquid, involved in the history of the differentiated asteroids giving us the nickel-iron meteorites, I did not worry about the fate of the basaltic liquids that should also have been formed near the middle of the heating event responsible. These issues show that a lot more work is still needed to understand the history of the asteroids fully (and some of it is already under way, of course). But they also illustrate just how fascinating the physical, as well as chemical, histories of the asteroids have been – at least as complex as those of the Earth and other planets!

Some Interesting Variable Stars

JOHN ISLES

The following stars are of interest for many reasons. Of course, the periods and ranges of many variables are not constant from one cycle to another.

Star	R.A. h	m	Declination deg.	min.	Range	Type	Period days	Spectrum
R Andromedæ	00	24.0	+38	35	5.8–14.9	Mira	409	S
W Andromedæ	02	17.6	+44	18	6.7–14.6	Mira	396	S
U Antliæ	10	35.2	−39	34	5–6	Irregular	–	C
Theta Apodis	14	05.3	−76	48	5–7	Semi-regular	119	M
R Aquarii	23	43.8	−15	17	5.8–12.4	Symbiotic	387	M+Pec
T Aquarii	20	49.9	−05	09	7.2–14.2	Mira	202	M
R Aquilæ	19	06.4	+08	14	5.5–12.0	Mira	284	M
V Aquilæ	19	04.4	−05	41	6.6– 8.4	Semi-regular	353	C
Eta Aquilæ	19	52.5	+01	00	3.5– 4.4	Cepheid	7.2	F–G
U Aræ	17	53.6	−51	41	7.7–14.1	Mira	225	M
R Arietis	02	16.1	+25	03	7.4–13.7	Mira	187	M
U Arietis	03	11.0	+14	48	7.2–15.2	Mira	371	M
R Aurigæ	05	17.3	+53	35	6.7–13.9	Mira	458	M
Epsilon Aurigæ	05	02.0	+43	49	2.9– 3.8	Algol	9892	F+B
R Boötis	14	37.2	+26	44	6.2–13.1	Mira	223	M
W Boötis	14	43.4	+26	32	4.7– 5.4	Semi-regular?	450?	M
X Camelopardalis	04	45.7	+75	06	7.4–14.2	Mira	144	K–M
R Cancri	08	16.6	+11	44	6.1–11.8	Mira	362	M
X Cancri	08	55.4	+17	14	5.6– 7.5	Semi-regular	195?	C
R Canis Majoris	07	19.5	−16	24	5.7– 6.3	Algol	1.1	F
S Canis Minoris	07	32.7	+08	19	6.6–13.2	Mira	333	M
R Canum Ven.	13	49.0	+39	33	6.5–12.9	Mira	329	M
R Carinæ	09	32.2	−62	47	3.9–10.5	Mira	309	M
S Carinæ	10	09.4	−61	33	4.5– 9.9	Mira	149	K–M
l Carinæ	09	45.2	−62	30	3.3– 4.2	Cepheid	35.5	F–K
Eta Carinæ	10	45.1	−59	41	−0.8– 7.9	Irregular	–	Pec
R Cassiopeiæ	23	58.4	+51	24	4.7–13.5	Mira	430	M
S Cassiopeiæ	01	19.7	+72	37	7.9–16.1	Mira	612	S
W Cassiopeiæ	00	54.9	+58	34	7.8–12.5	Mira	406	C
Gamma Cass.	00	56.7	+60	43	1.6– 3.0	Irregular	–	B
Rho Cassiopeiæ	23	54.4	+57	30	4.1– 6.2	Semi-regular	–	F–K
R Centauri	14	16.6	−59	55	5.3–11.8	Mira	546	M
S Centauri	12	24.6	−49	26	7–8	Semi-regular	65	C
T Centauri	13	41.8	−33	36	5.5– 9.0	Semi-regular	90	K–M
S Cephei	21	35.2	+78	37	7.4–12.9	Mira	487	C
T Cephei	21	09.5	+68	29	5.2–11.3	Mira	388	M
Delta Cephei	22	29.2	+58	25	3.5– 4.4	Cepheid	5.4	F–G
Mu Cephei	21	43.5	+58	47	3.4– 5.1	Semi-regular	730	M
U Ceti	02	33.7	−13	09	6.8–13.4	Mira	235	M
W Ceti	00	02.1	−14	41	7.1–14.8	Mira	351	S
Omicron Ceti	02	19.3	−02	59	2.0–10.1	Mira	332	M

Star	R.A. h	m	Declination deg.	min.	Range	Type	Period days	Spectrum
R Chamælcontis	08	21.8	−76	21	7.5–14.2	Mira	335	M
T Columbæ	05	19.3	−33	42	6.6–12.7	Mira	226	M
R Comæ Ber.	12	04.3	+18	47	7.1–14.6	Mira	363	M
R Coronæ Bor.	15	48.6	+28	09	5.7–14.8	R Coronæ Bor.	–	C
S Coronæ Bor.	15	21.4	+31	22	5.8–14.1	Mira	360	M
T Coronæ Bor.	15	59.6	+25	55	2.0–10.8	Recurr. nova	–	M+Pec
V Coronæ Bor.	15	49.5	+39	34	6.9–12.6	Mira	358	C
W Coronæ Bor.	16	15.4	+37	48	7.8–14.3	Mira	238	M
R Corvi	12	19.6	−19	15	6.7–14.4	Mira	317	M
R Crucis	12	23.6	−61	38	6.4– 7.2	Cepheid	5.8	F–G
R Cygni	19	36.8	+50	12	6.1–14.4	Mira	426	S
U Cygni	20	19.6	+47	54	5.9–12.1	Mira	463	C
W Cygni	21	36.0	+45	22	5.0– 7.6	Semi-regular	131	M
RT Cygni	19	43.6	+48	47	6.0–13.1	Mira	190	M
SS Cygni	21	42.7	+43	35	7.7–12.4	Dwarf nova	50±	K+Pec
CH Cygni	19	24.5	+50	14	5.6– 9.0	Symbiotic	–	M+B
Chi Cygni	19	50.6	+32	55	3.3–14.2	Mira	408	S
R Delphini	20	14.9	+09	05	7.6–13.8	Mira	285	M
U Delphini	20	45.5	+18	05	5.6– 7.5	Semi-regular	110?	M
EU Delphini	20	37.9	+18	16	5.8– 6.9	Semi-regular	60	M
Beta Doradus	05	33.6	−62	29	3.5– 4.1	Cepheid	9.8	F–G
R Draconis	16	32.7	+66	45	6.7–13.2	Mira	246	M
T Eridani	03	55.2	−24	02	7.2–13.2	Mira	252	M
R Fornacis	02	29.3	−26	06	7.5–13.0	Mira	389	C
R Geminorum	07	07.4	+22	42	6.0–14.0	Mira	370	S
U Geminorum	07	55.1	+22	00	8.2–14.9	Dwarf nova	105±	Pec+M
Zeta Geminorum	07	04.1	+20	34	3.6– 4.2	Cepheid	10.2	F–G
Eta Geminorum	06	14.9	+22	30	3.2– 3.9	Semi-regular	233	M
S Gruis	22	26.1	−48	26	6.0–15.0	Mira	402	M
S Herculis	16	51.9	+14	56	6.4–13.8	Mira	307	M
U Herculis	16	25.8	+18	54	6.4–13.4	Mira	406	M
Alpha Herculis	17	14.6	+14	23	2.7– 4.0	Semi-regular	–	M
68, u Herculis	17	17.3	+33	06	4.7– 5.4	Algol	2.1	B+B
R Horologii	02	53.9	−49	53	4.7–14.3	Mira	408	M
U Horologii	03	52.8	−45	50	6–14	Mira	348	M
R Hydræ	13	29.7	−23	17	3.5–10.9	Mira	389	M
U Hydræ	10	37.6	−13	23	4.3– 6.5	Semi-regular	450?	C
VW Hydri	04	09.1	−71	18	8.4–14.4	Dwarf nova	27±	Pec
R Leonis	09	47.6	+11	26	4.4–11.3	Mira	310	M
R Leonis Minoris	09	45.6	+34	31	6.3–13.2	Mira	372	M
R Leporis	04	59.6	−14	48	5.5–11.7	Mira	427	C
Y Libræ	15	11.7	−06	01	7.6–14.7	Mira	276	M
RS Libræ	15	24.3	−22	55	7.0–13.0	Mira	218	M
Delta Libræ	15	01.0	−08	31	4.9– 5.9	Algol	2.3	A
R Lyncis	07	01.3	+55	20	7.2–14.3	Mira	379	S
R Lyræ	18	55.3	+43	57	3.9– 5.0	Semi-regular	46?	M
RR Lyræ	19	25.5	+42	47	7.1– 8.1	RR Lyræ	0.6	A–F
Beta Lyræ	18	50.1	+33	22	3.3– 4.4	Eclipsing	12.9	B
U Microscopii	20	29.2	−40	25	7.0–14.4	Mira	334	M
U Monocerotis	07	30.8	−09	47	5.9– 7.8	RV Tauri	91	F–K
V Monocerotis	06	22.7	−02	12	6.0–13.9	Mira	340	M
R Normæ	15	36.0	−49	30	6.5–13.9	Mira	508	M
T Normæ	15	44.1	−54	59	6.2–13.6	Mira	241	M
R Octantis	05	26.1	−86	23	6.3–13.2	Mira	405	M
S Octantis	18	08.7	−86	48	7.2–14.0	Mira	259	M
V Ophiuchi	16	26.7	−12	26	7.3–11.6	Mira	297	C
X Ophiuchi	18	38.3	+08	50	5.9– 9.2	Mira	329	M
RS Ophiuchi	17	50.2	−06	43	4.3–12.5	Recurr. nova	–	OB+M
U Orionis	05	55.8	+20	10	4.8–13.0	Mira	368	M
W Orionis	05	05.4	+01	11	5.9– 7.7	Semi-regular	212	C

Star	R.A. h	m	Declination deg.	min.	Range	Type	Period days	Spectrum
Alpha Orionis	05	55.2	+07	24	0.0– 1.3	Semi-regular	2335	M
S Pavonis	19	55.2	−59	12	6.6–10.4	Semi-regular	381	M
Kappa Pavonis	18	56.9	−67	14	3.9– 4.8	Cepheid	9.1	G
R Pegasi	23	06.8	+10	33	6.9–13.8	Mira	378	M
Beta Pegasi	23	03.8	+28	05	2.3– 2.7	Irregular	–	M
X Persei	03	55.4	+31	03	6.0– 7.0	Gamma Cass.	–	O9.5
Beta Persei	03	08.2	+40	57	2.1– 3.4	Algol	2.9	B
Rho Persei	03	05.2	+38	50	3.3– 4.0	Semi-regular	50?	M
Zeta Phœnicis	01	08.4	−55	15	3.9– 4.4	Algol	1.7	B+B
R Pictoris	04	46.2	−49	15	6.4–10.1	Semi-regular	171	M
L² Puppis	07	13.5	−44	39	2.6– 6.2	Semi-regular	141	M
T Pyxidis	09	04.7	−32	23	6.5–15.3	Recurr. nova	7000±	Pec
U Sagittæ	19	18.8	+19	37	6.5– 9.3	Algol	3.4	B+G
WZ Sagittæ	20	07.6	+17	42	7.0–15.5	Dwarf nova	11900±	A
R Sagittarii	19	16.7	−19	18	6.7–12.8	Mira	270	M
RR Sagittarii	19	55.9	−29	11	5.4–14.0	Mira	336	M
RT Sagittarii	20	17.7	−39	07	6.0–14.1	Mira	306	M
RU Sagittarii	19	58.7	−41	51	6.0–13.8	Mira	240	M
RY Sagittarii	19	16.5	−33	31	5.8–14.0	R Coronæ Bor.	–	G
RR Scorpii	16	56.6	−30	35	5.0–12.4	Mira	281	M
RS Scorpii	16	55.6	−45	06	6.2–13.0	Mira	320	M
RT Scorpii	17	03.5	−36	55	7.0–15.2	Mira	449	S
S Sculptoris	00	15.4	−32	03	5.5–13.6	Mira	363	M
R Scuti	18	47.5	−05	42	4.2– 8.6	RV Tauri	146	G–K
R Serpentis	15	50.7	+15	08	5.2–14.4	Mira	356	M
S Serpentis	15	21.7	+14	19	7.0–14.1	Mira	372	M
T Tauri	04	22.0	+19	32	9.3–13.5	Irregular	–	F–K
SU Tauri	05	49.1	+19	04	9.1–16.9	R Coronæ Bor.	–	G
Lambda Tauri	04	00.7	+12	29	3.4– 3.9	Algol	4.0	B+A
R Trianguli	02	37.0	+34	16	5.4–12.6	Mira	267	M
R Ursæ Majoris	10	44.6	+68	47	6.5–13.7	Mira	302	M
T Ursæ Majoris	12	36.4	+59	29	6.6–13.5	Mira	257	M
U Ursæ Minoris	14	17.3	+66	48	7.1–13.0	Mira	331	M
R Virginis	12	38.5	+06	59	6.1–12.1	Mira	146	M
S Virginis	13	33.0	−07	12	6.3–13.2	Mira	375	M
SS Virginis	12	25.3	+00	48	6.0– 9.6	Semi-regular	364	C
R Vulpeculæ	21	04.4	+23	49	7.0–14.3	Mira	137	M
Z Vulpeculæ	19	21.7	+25	34	7.3– 8.9	Algol	2.5	B+A

Mira Stars: maxima, 1995

JOHN ISLES

Below are given predicted dates of maxima for Mira stars that reach magnitude 7.5 or brighter at an average maximum. Individual maxima can in some cases be brighter or fainter than average by a magnitude or more, and all dates are only approximate. The positions, extreme ranges and mean periods of these stars can all be found in the preceding list of interesting variable stars.

Star	Mean magnitude at maximum	Dates of maxima
W Andromedæ	7.4	Apr. 1
R Aquarii	6.5	Feb. 7
R Aquilæ	6.1	Jan. 18, Oct. 30
R Boötis	7.2	Mar. 22, Oct. 31
R Cancri	6.8	Oct. 30
S Canis Minoris	7.5	June 30
R Carinæ	4.6	Jan. 18, Nov. 23
S Carinæ	5.7	Apr. 8, Sep. 5
R Cassiopeiæ	7.0	Nov. 3
R Centauri	5.8	June 21
T Cephei	6.0	Dec. 29
U Ceti	7.5	Mar. 5, Oct. 25
Omicron Ceti	3.4	May 16
T Columbæ	7.5	Feb. 12, Sep. 26
S Coronæ Borealis	7.3	Oct. 11
V Coronæ Borealis	7.5	May 11
R Corvi	7.5	Mar. 23
U Cygni	7.2	Oct. 4
RT Cygni	7.3	June 21, Dec. 28
Chi Cygni	5.2	May 31
R Geminorum	7.1	Oct. 21
U Herculis	7.5	Apr. 28
R Horologii	6.0	July 4
U Horologii	7	Mar. 1
R Hydræ	4.5	Jan. 30
R Leonis	5.8	May 12
R Leonis Minoris	7.1	Aug. 7
R Leporis	6.8	Apr. 27
RS Libræ	7.5	July 26
V Monocerotis	7.0	Oct. 26
T Normæ	7.4	Apr. 26, Dec. 23

Star	Mean magnitude at maximum	Dates of maxima
V Ophiuchi	7.5	July 24
X Ophiuchi	6.8	Feb. 6
U Orionis	6.3	Nov. 17
R Sagittarii	7.3	June 29
RR Sagittarii	6.8	May 3
RT Sagittarii	7.0	Mar. 30
RU Sagittarii	7.2	Jan. 7, Sep. 4
RR Scorpii	5.9	Sep. 22
RS Scorpii	7.0	Apr. 15
S Sculptoris	6.7	Nov. 29
R Serpentis	6.9	Mar. 25
R Trianguli	6.2	May 28
R Ursæ Majoris	7.5	May 24
R Virginis	6.9	Jan. 14, June 9, Nov. 1
S Virginis	7.0	Aug. 29

Some Interesting Double Stars

R. W. ARGYLE

The positions given below correspond to epoch 1995.0

Name	Magnitudes	Separation in seconds of arc	Position angle, degrees	Notes
Gamma Andromedæ	2.3, 5.0	9.4	064	Yellow, blue. B is again double.
Zeta Aquarii	4.3, 4.5	2.0	196	Slowly widening.
Gamma Arietis	4.8, 4.8	7.6	000	Very easy. Both white.
Epsilon Arietis	5.2, 5.5	1.5	208	Binary. Both white.
Theta Aurigæ	2.6, 7.1	3.7	310	Stiff test for 3-in.
44 Boötis	5.3, 6.2	2.0	051	Period 246 years.
Xi Boötis	4.7, 7.0	6.9	322	Fine contrast. Easy.
Epsilon Boötis	2.5, 4.9	2.8	342	Yellow, blue. Fine pair.
Zeta Cancri	5.6, 6.2	6.0	074	A again double.
Iota Cancri	4.2, 6.6	30.4	307	Easy. Yellow, blue.
Alpha Canum Ven.	2.9, 5.5	19.6	228	Easy. Yellow, bluish.
Upsilon Carinæ	3.1, 6.1	5.0	127	Fixed.
Eta Cassiopeiæ	3.4, 7.5	12.7	315	Easy. Creamy, bluish.
Alpha Centauri	0.0, 1.2	17.3	218	Very easy. Period 80 years.
Gamma Centauri	2.9, 2.9	1.2	351	Period 84 years. Closing. Both yellow.
3 Centauri	4.5, 6.0	7.8	105	Both white.
Beta Cephei	3.2, 7.9	14	250	Easy with a 3-in.
Delta Cephei	var, 7.5	41	192	Very easy.
Xi Cephei	4.4, 6.5	8.0	276	White, blue.
Gamma Ceti	3.5, 7.3	2.9	294	Not too easy.
Alpha Circini	3.2, 8.6	15.7	230	PA slowly decreasing.
Zeta Corona Bor.	5.1, 6.0	6.3	305	PA slowly increasing.
Delta Corvi	3.0, 9.2	24	214	Easy with a 3-in.
Alpha Crucis	1.4, 1.9	4.2	114	Third star in a low-power field.
Gamma Crucis	1.6, 6.7	124	024	Third star in a low-power field.
Mu Crucis	4.3, 5.3	34.9	017	Fixed. Both white.
Beta Cygni	3.1, 5.1	34.1	054	Glorious. Yellow, blue.
61 Cygni	5.2, 6.0	30.2	149	Nearby binary. Period 722 years.
Gamma Delphini	4.5, 5.5	9.3	267	Easy. Yellowish, greenish.
Epsilon Draconis	3.8, 7.4	3.2	019	Slow binary.
Nu Draconis	4.9, 4.9	62	312	Naked eye pair.
f Eridani	4.8, 5.3	8.2	215	Pale yellow.
p Eridani	5.8, 5.8	11.4	192	Period 483 years.
Theta Eridani	3.4, 4.5	8.3	090	Both white.

Name	Magnitudes	Separation in seconds of arc	Position angle, degrees	Notes
Alpha Geminorum	1.9, 2.9	3.5	072	Widening. Easy with a 3-in.
Delta Geminorum	3.5, 8.2	5.9	224	Not too easy.
Alpha Herculis	var, 5.4	4.6	106	Red, green. Binary.
Delta Herculis	3.1, 8.2	10.4	276	Optical pair. Distance increasing.
Zeta Herculis	2.9, 5.5	1.4	061	Fine, rapid binary. Period 34 years.
Epsilon Hydræ	3.3, 6.8	2.7	298	PA slowly increasing.
Theta Indi	4.5, 7.0	6.7	266	Fine contrast.
Gamma Leonis	2.2, 3.5	4.4	125	Binary, 619 years.
Pi Lupi	4.6, 4.7	1.7	065	Widening.
Alpha Lyræ	0.0, 9.5	76	182	Optical pair. B is faint.
Epsilon¹ Lyr	5.0, 6.1	2.6	352	Quadruple system. Both
Epsilon² Lyr	5.2, 5.5	2.3	085	pairs visible in a 3-in.
Zeta Lyræ	4.3, 5.9	44	149	Fixed. Easy double.
Beta Muscæ	3.7, 4.0	1.3	039	Both white.
70 Ophiuchi	4.2, 6.0	2.5	168	Rapid motion.
Beta Orionis	0.1, 6.8	9.5	202	Can be seen with 3-in.
Iota Orionis	2.8, 6.9	11.8	141	Enmeshed in nebulosity.
Theta Orionis	6.7, 7.9	8.7	032	Trapezium in M42.
	5.1, 6.7	13.4	061	
Sigma Orionis	4.0, 10.3	11.4	238	Quintuple. A is a
	6.5, 7.5	30.1	231	close double.
Zeta Orionis	1.9, 4.0	2.4	162	Can be split in 3-in.
Xi Pavonis	4.4, 8.6	3.3	155	Orange and white.
Eta Persei	3.8, 8.5	28.5	300	Yellow, bluish.
Beta Phœnicis	4.0, 4.2	1.5	324	Slowly widening.
Beta Piscis Aust.	4.4, 7.9	30.4	172	Optical pair. Fixed.
Alpha Piscium	4.2, 5.1	1.9	275	Binary, 933 years.
Kappa Puppis	4.5, 4.7	9.8	318	Both white.
Alpha Scorpii	1.2, 5.4	2.7	274	Red, green.
Nu Scorpii	4.3, 6.4	42	336	Both again double.
Theta Serpentis	4.5, 5.4	22.3	103	Fixed. Very easy.
Alpha Tauri	0.9, 11.1	131	032	Wide, but B very faint in small telescopes.
Iota Trianguli	5.3, 6.9	3.9	070	Slow binary.
Beta Tucanæ	4.4, 4.8	27.1	170	Both again double.
Delta Tucanæ	4.5, 9.0	6.9	282	White, reddish.
Zeta Ursæ Majoris	2.3, 4.0	14.4	151	Very easy. Naked eye pair with Alcor.
Xi Ursæ Majoris	4.3, 4.8	1.1	317	Binary, 60 years. Opening. Needs a 4-in.
Delta Velorum	2.1, 5.1	2.0	140	Slowly closing.
s Velorum	6.2, 6.5	13.5	218	Fixed.
Gamma Virginis	3.5, 3.5	2.2	277	Binary, 168 years. Closing.
Theta Virginis	4.4, 9.4	7.1	343	Not too easy.
Gamma Volantis	3.9, 5.8	13.8	299	Very slow binary.

Some Interesting Nebulæ and Clusters

Object	R.A.		Dec.		Remarks
	h	*m*			
M.31 Andromedæ	00	40.7	+41	05	Great Galaxy, visible to naked eye.
H.VIII 78 Cassiopeiæ	00	41.3	+61	36	Fine cluster, between Gamma and Kappa Cassiopeiæ.
M.33 Trianguli	01	31.8	+30	28	Spiral. Difficult with small apertures.
H.VI 33–4 Persei	02	18.3	+56	59	Double cluster; Sword-handle.
△142 Doradûs	05	39.1	−69	09	Looped nebula round 30 Doradûs. Naked-eye. In Large Cloud of Magellan.
M.1 Tauri	05	32.3	+22	00	Crab Nebula, near Zeta Tauri.
M.42 Orionis	05	33.4	−05	24	Great Nebula. Contains the famous Trapezium, Theta Orionis.
M.35 Geminorum	06	06.5	+24	21	Open cluster near Eta Geminorum.
H.VII 2 Monocerotis	06	30.7	+04	53	Open cluster, just visible to naked eye.
M.41 Canis Majoris	06	45.5	−20	42	Open cluster, just visible to naked eye.
M.47 Puppis	07	34.3	−14	22	Mag. 5,2. Loose cluster.
H.IV 64 Puppis	07	39.6	−18	05	Bright planetary in rich neighbourhood.
M.46 Puppis	07	39.5	−14	42	Open cluster.
M.44 Cancri	08	38	+20	07	Præsepe. Open cluster near Delta Cancri. Visible to naked eye.
M.97 Ursæ Majoris	11	12.6	+55	13	Owl Nebula, diameter 3'. Planetary.
Kappa Crucis	12	50.7	−60	05	'Jewel Box'; open cluster, with stars of contrasting colours.
M.3 Can. Ven.	13	40.6	+28	34	Bright globular.
Omega Centauri	13	23.7	−47	03	Finest of all globulars. Easy with naked eye.
M.80 Scorpii	16	14.9	−22	53	Globular, between Antares and Beta Scorpionis.
M.4 Scorpii	16	21.5	−26	26	Open cluster close to Antares.
M.13 Herculis	16	40	+36	31	Globular. Just visible to naked eye.
M.92 Herculis	16	16.1	+43	11	Globular. Between Iota and Eta Herculis.
M.6 Scorpii	17	36.8	−32	11	Open cluster; naked eye.
M.7 Scorpii	17	50.6	−34	48	Very bright open cluster; naked eye.
M.23 Sagittarii	17	54.8	−19	01	Open cluster nearly 50' in diameter.
H.IV 37 Draconis	17	58.6	+66	38	Bright planetary.
M.8 Sagittarii	18	01.4	−24	23	Lagoon Nebula. Gaseous. Just visible with naked eye.
NGC 6572 Ophiuchi	18	10.9	+06	50	Bright planetary, between Beta Ophiuchi and Zeta Aquilæ.
M.17 Sagittarii	18	18.8	−16	12	Omega Nebula. Gaseous. Large and bright.
M.11 Scuti	18	49.0	−06	19	Wild Duck. Bright open cluster.
M.57 Lyræ	18	52.6	+32	59	Ring Nebula. Brightest of planetaries.
M.27 Vulpeculæ	19	58.1	+22	37	Dumb-bell Nebula, near Gamma Sagittæ.
H.IV 1 Aquarii	21	02.1	−11	31	Bright planetary near Nu Aquarii.
M.15 Pegasi	21	28.3	+12	01	Bright globular, near Epsilon Pegasi.
M.39 Cygni	21	31.0	+48	17	Open cluster between Deneb and Alpha Lacertæ. Well seen with low powers.

Our Contributors

Dr David Allen continued his work at Siding Spring Observatory, but readers of the *Yearbook* will be sorry to know that he sadly died in July.

Dr Paul Murdin has returned to Cambridge, following his period as Director of the Royal Observatory Edinburgh, and continues to make major contributions to astrophysics.

Dr Phil Charles, of Oxford University, has been paying special attention to X-ray binaries and the search for black holes; much of his observation is carried out with the William Herschel Telescope on La Palma.

Dr Ron Maddison, who emigrated from Keele University to Merritt Island some years ago, is in charge of the Planetarium there, and is also very active in general astronomical education. From his home he can watch rockets ascending from Cape Canaveral!

Charles Gordon-Graham graduated from York University, and obtained his Master's Degree at Sussex University. His particular interests include variable stars, stellar evolution, and the history of astronomy. He is at present Lecturer in Astronomy at Ercites University in Turkey.

Dr Fred Watson spent some years at Siding Spring in Australia, but has now returned to the United Kingdom, and is currently at Cambridge. He is one of the main pioneers of the development of fibre optics for astronomy.

Professor Iwan Williams is Professor of Astronomy at Queen Mary and Westfield College, University of London. He is particularly interested in asteroids, meteoroids, and comets.

Professor Lionel Wilson, of the University of Lancaster, has specialized in Solar System studies, and has made many major contributions to this field of research.

The William Herschel Society maintains the museum now established at 19 New King Street, Bath – the only surviving Herschel House. It also undertakes activities of various kinds. New members would be welcome; those interested are asked to contact Dr L. Hilliard at 2 Lambridge, London Road, Bath.

Astronomical Societies in Great Britain

British Astronomical Association
Assistant Secretary: Burlington House, Piccadilly, London W1V 9AG.
Meetings: Lecture Hall of Scientific Societies, Civil Service Commission Building, 23 Savile Row, London W1. Last Wednesday each month (Oct.–June). 1700 hrs and some Saturday afternoons.

Association for Astronomy Education
Secretary: Bob Kibble, 34 Ackland Crescent, Denmark Hill, London SE5 8EQ.

Astronomy Ireland
Secretary: Antoinette Moore, PO Box 2888, Dublin 1.
Meetings: Ely House, 8 Ely Place, Dublin 2. 8 p.m., 2nd and 4th Mondays of each month September–April.

Astronomical Society of Wales
Secretary: John Minopoli, 12 Gwendoline Street, Port Talbot, West Glamorgan.

Federation of Astronomical Societies
Secretary: Mrs Christine Sheldon, Whitehaven, Lower Moor, Pershore, Worcs.

Junior Astronomical Society
Secretary: Guy Fennimore, 36 Fairway, Keyworth, Nottingham.
Meetings: London. Last Saturday Jan., April, July, Oct. 2.30 p.m. Details from Secretary.

Junior Astronomical Society of Ireland
Secretary: K. Nolan, 5 St Patrick's Crescent, Rathcoole, Co. Dublin.
Meetings: The Royal Dublin Society, Ballsbridge, Dublin 4. Monthly.

Aberdeen and District Astronomical Society
Secretary: Stephen Graham, 25 Davidson Place, Northfield, Aberdeen.
Meetings: Robert Gordon's Institute of Technology, St Andrew's Street, Aberdeen. Friday 7.30 p.m.

Altrincham and District Astronomical Society
Secretary: Colin Henshaw, 10 Delamore Road, Gatley, Cheadle, Cheshire.
Meetings: Public Library, Timperley. 1st Friday of each month, 7.30 p.m.

Astra Astronomy Section
Secretary: Ian Downie, 151 Sword Street, Glasgow G31.
Meetings: Public Library, Airdrie. Weekly.

Aylesbury Astronomical Society
Secretary: Nigel Sheridan, 22 Moor Park, Wendover, Bucks.
Meetings: 1st Monday in month. Details from Secretary.

Bassetlaw Astronomical Society
Secretary: H. Marlson, 5 Magnolia Close, South Aston, South Yorks.
Meetings: Rockware Glass, Sports & Social Club, Sandy Lane, Worksop, Notts. Tuesday fortnightly, 7.30 p.m.

Batley & Spenborough Astronomical Society
Secretary: Robert Morton, 22 Links Avenue, Cleckheaton, West Yorks BD19 4EG.
Meetings: Milner K. Ford Observatory, Wilton Park, Batley. Every Thursday, 7.30 p.m.

Bedford Astronomical Society
Secretary: D. Eagle, 24 Copthorne Close, Oakley, Bedford.
Meetings: Bedford School, Burnaby Rd, Bedford. Last Tuesday each month.

Bingham & Brookes Space Organization
Secretary: N. Bingham, 15 Hickmore's Lane, Lindfield, W. Sussex.

Birmingham Astronomical Society
Secretary: J. Spittles, 28 Milverton Road, Knowle, Solihull, West Midlands.
Meetings: Room 146, Aston University, last Tuesday each month, Sept. to June (except December moved to 1st week in January).

Blackpool & District Astronomical Society
Secretary: J. L. Crossley, 24 Fernleigh Close, Bispham, Blackpool, Lancs.

Bolton Astronomical Society
Secretary: Peter Miskiw, 9 Hedley Street, Bolton.

Border Astronomical Society
Secretary: David Pettit, 14 Shap Grove, Carlisle, Cumbria.

Boston Astronomers
Secretary: B. Tongue, South View, Fen Road, Stickford, Boston.
Meetings: Details from the Secretary.

Bradford Astronomical Society
Secretary: John Schofield, Briar Lea, Bromley Road, Bingley, W. Yorks.
Meetings: Eccleshill Library, Bradford 2. Monday fortnightly (with occasional variations).

Braintree, Halstead & District Astronomical Society
Secretary: Heather Reeder, The Knoll, St Peters in the Field, Braintree, Essex.
Meetings: St Peter's Church Hall, St Peter's Road, Braintree, Essex. 3rd Thursday each month, 8 p.m.

Bridgend Amateur Astronomical Society
Secretary: J. M. Pugsley, 32 Hoel Fawr, Broadlands, North Cornelly, Bridgend.
Meetings: G.P. Room, Recreation Centre, Bridgend, 1st and 3rd Friday monthly, 7.30 p.m.

Bridgwater Astronomical Society
Secretary: W. L. Buckland, 104 Polden Street, Bridgwater, Somerset.
Meetings: Room D10, Bridgwater College, Bath Road Centre, Bridgwater. 2nd Wednesday each month, Sept.–June.

Brighton Astronomical Society
Secretary: Mrs B. C. Smith, Flat 2, 23 Albany Villas, Hove, Sussex BN3 2RS.
Meetings: Preston Tennis Club, Preston Drive, Brighton. Weekly, Tuesdays.

Bristol Astronomical Society
Secretary: Y. A. Sage, 33 Mackie Avenue, Filton, Bristol.
Meetings: Royal Fort (Rm G44), Bristol University. Every Friday each month, Sept.–May. Fortnightly, June–August.

Cambridge Astronomical Association
Secretary: R. J. Greening, 20 Cotts Croft, Great Chishill, Royston, Herts.
Meetings: Venues as published in newsletter. 1st and 3rd Friday each month, 8 p.m.

Cardiff Astronomical Society
Secretary: D. W. S. Powell, 1 Tal-y-Bont Road, Ely, Cardiff.
Meeting Place: Room 230, Dept. Law, University College, Museum Avenue, Cardiff. Alternate Thursdays, 8 p.m.

Castle Point Astronomy Club
Secretary: Miss Zena White, 43 Lambeth Road, Eastwood, Essex.
Meetings: St Michael's Church, Thundersley. Most Wednesdays, 8 p.m.

Chelmsford Astronomers
Secretary: Brendan Clark, 5 Borda Close, Chelmsford, Essex.
Meetings: Once a month.

Chelmsford and District Astronomical Society
Secretary: Miss C. C. Puddick, 6 Walpole Walk, Rayleigh, Essex.
Meetings: Sandon House School, Sandon, near Chelmsford. 2nd and last Monday of month. 7.45 p.m.

Chester Astronomical Society
Secretary: Mrs S. Brooks, 39 Halton Road, Great Sutton, South Wirral.
Meetings: Southview Community Centre, Southview Road, Chester. Last Monday each month except Aug. and Dec., 7.30 p.m.

Chester Society of Natural Science Literature and Art
Secretary: Paul Braid, 'White Wing', 38 Bryn Avenue, Old Colwyn, Colwyn Bay, Clwyd.
Meetings: Grosvenor Museum, Chester. Fortnightly.

Chesterfield Astronomical Society
Secretary: P. Lisewski, 148 Old Hall Road, Brampton, Chesterfield.
Meetings: Barnet Observatory, Newbold. Each Friday.

Clacton & District Astronomical Society
Secretary: C. L. Haskell, 105 London Road, Clacton-on-Sea, Essex.

Cleethorpes & District Astronomical Society
Secretary: C. Illingworth, 38 Shaw Drive, Grimsby, S. Humberside.
Meetings: Beacon Hill Observatory, Cleethorpes. 1st Wednesday each month.

Cleveland & Darlington Astronomical Society
Secretary: Neil Haggath, 5 Fountains Crescent, Eston, Middlesbrough, Cleveland.
Meetings: Elmwood Community Centre, Greens Lane, Hartburn, Stockton-on-Tees. Monthly, usually 2nd Friday.

Colchester Amateur Astronomers
Secretary: F. Kelly, 'Middleton', Church Road, Elmstead Market, Colchester, Essex.
Meetings: William Loveless Hall, High Street, Wivenhoe. Friday evenings. Fortnightly.

Cotswold Astronomical Society
Secretary: Trevor Talbot, Innisfree, Winchcombe Road, Sedgebarrow, Worcs.
Meetings: Fortnightly in Cheltenham or Gloucester.

Coventry & Warwicks Astronomical Society
Secretary: V. Cooper, 5 Gisburn Close, Woodloes Park, Warwick.
Meetings: Coventry Technical College. 1st Friday each month, Sept.–June.

Crawley Astronomical Society
Secretary: G. Cowley, 67 Climpixy Road, Ifield, Crawley, Sussex.
Meetings: Crawley College of Further Education. Monthly Oct.–June.

Crayford Manor House Astronomical Society
Secretary: R. H. Chambers, Manor House Centre, Crayford, Kent.
Meetings: Manor House Centre, Crayford. Monthly during term-time.

Croydon Astronomical Society
Secretary: Simon Bailey, 39 Sanderstead Road, South Croydon, Surrey.
Meetings: Lecture Theatre, Royal Russell School, Combe Lane, South Croydon. Alternate Fridays, 7.45 p.m.
Derby & District Astronomical Society
Secretary: Jane D. Kirk, 7 Cromwell Avenue, Findern, Derby.
Meetings: At home of Secretary. 1st and 3rd Friday each month, 7.30 p.m.
Doncaster Astronomical Society
Secretary: J. A. Day, 297 Lonsdale Avenue, Intake, Doncaster.
Meetings: Fridays, weekly.
Dundee Astronomical Society
Secretary: G. Young, 37 Polepark Road, Dundee, Angus.
Meetings: Mills Observatory, Balgay Park, Dundee. 1st Friday each month, 7.30 p.m. Sept.–April.
Easington and District Astronomical Society
Secretary: T. Bradley, 52 Jameson Road, Hartlepool, Co. Durham.
Meetings: Easington Comprehensive School, Easington Colliery. Every 3rd Thursday throughout the year, 7.30 p.m.
Eastbourne Astronomical Society
Secretary: D. C. Gates, Apple Tree Cottage, Stunts Green, Hertsmonceux, East Sussex.
Meetings: St Aiden's Church Hall, 1 Whitley Road, Eastbourne. Monthly (except July and August).
East Lancashire Astronomical Society
Secretary: D. Chadwick, 16 Worston Lane, Great Harwood, Blackburn BB6 7TH.
Meetings: As arranged. Monthly.
Astronomical Society of Edinburgh
Secretary: R. G. Fenoulhet, 7 Greenend Gardens, Edinburgh EH17 7QB.
Meetings: City Observatory, Calton Hill, Edinburgh. Monthly.
Edinburgh University Astronomical Society
Secretary: c/o Dept. of Astronomy, Royal Observatory, Blackford Hill, Edinburgh.
Ewell Astronomical Society
Secretary: Edward Hanna, 91 Tennyson Avenue, Motspur Park, Surrey.
Meetings: 1st Friday of each month.
Exeter Astronomical Society
Secretary: Miss J. Corey, 5 Egham Avenue, Topsham Road, Exeter.
Meetings: The Meeting Room, Wynards, Magdalen Street, Exeter. 1st Thursday of month.
Farnham Astronomical Society
Secretary: Laurence Anslow, 14 Wellington Lane, Farnham, Surrey.
Meetings: Church House, Union Road, Farnham. 2nd Monday each month, 7.45 p.m.
Fitzharry's Astronomical Society (Oxford & District)
Secretary: Mark Harman, 20 Lapwing Lane, Cholsey, Oxon.
Meetings: All Saints Methodist Church, Dorchester Crescent, Abingdon, Oxon.
Forest Astronomical Society
Chairman: Tony Beale, 8 Mill Lane, Lower Beeding, West Sussex.
Meetings: 1st Wednesday each month, juniors following Fridays. For location contact chairman.
Furness Astronomical Society
Secretary: A. Thompson, 52 Ocean Road, Walney Island, Barrow-in-Furness, Cumbria.
Meetings: St Mary's Church Centre, Dalton-in-Furness. 2nd Saturday in month, 7.30 p.m. No August meeting.
Fylde Astronomical Society
Secretary: 28 Belvedere Road, Thornton, Lancs.
Meetings: Stanley Hall, Rossendale Avenue South. 1st Wednesday each month.
Astronomical Society of Glasgow
Secretary: Malcolm Kennedy, 32 Cedar Road, Cumbernauld, Glasgow.
Meetings: University of Strathclyde, George St., Glasgow. 3rd Thursday each month, Sept.–April.
Greenock Astronomical Society
Secretary: Carl Hempsey, 49 Brisbane Street, Greenock.
Meetings: Greenock Arts Guild, 3 Campbell Street, Greenock.
Grimsby Astronomical Society
Secretary: R. Williams, 14 Richmond Close, Grimsby, South Humberside.
Meetings: Secretary's home. 2nd Thursday each month, 7.30 p.m.
Guernsey: La Société Guernesiaise Astronomy Section
Secretary: G. Falla, Highcliffe, Avenue Beauvais, Ville du Roi, St Peter's Port, Guernsey.
Meetings: The Observatory, St Peter's, Tuesdays, 8 p.m.
Guildford Astronomical Society
Secretary: A. Langmaid, 22 West Mount, Guildford, Surrey.
Meetings: Guildford Institute, Ward Street, Guildford. 1st Thursday each month, except July and August, 7.30 p.m.
Gwynedd Astronomical Society
Secretary: P. J. Curtis, Ael-y-bryn, Malltraeth St Newborough, Anglesey, Gwynedd.
Meetings: Physics Lecture Room, Bangor University. 1st Thursday each month, 7.30 p.m.

The Hampshire Astronomical Group
   Secretary: R. F. Dodd, 1 Conifer Close, Cowplain, Waterlooville, Hants.
   Meetings: Clanfield Observatory. Each Friday, 7.30 p.m.
Astronomical Society of Haringey
   Secretary: Wally Baker, 58 Stirling Road, Wood Green, London N22.
   Meetings: The Hall of the Good Shepherd, Berwick Road, Wood Green. 3rd Wednesday each month, 8 p.m.
Harrogate Astronomical Society
   Secretary: P. Barton, 31 Gordon Avenue, Harrogate, North Yorkshire.
   Meetings: Harlow Hill Methodist Church Hall, 121 Otley Road, Harrogate. Last Friday each month.
Heart of England Astronomical Society
   Secretary: Jean Poyner, 67 Ellerton Road, Kingstanding, Birmingham B44 0QE.
   Meetings: Furnace End Village, every Thursday.
Hebden Bridge Literary & Scientific Society, Astronomical Section
   Secretary: F. Parker, 48 Caldene Avenue, Mytholmroyd, Hebden Bridge, West Yorkshire.
Herschel Astronomy Society
   Secretary: D. R. Whittaker, 149 Farnham Lane, Slough.
   Meetings: Eton College, 2nd Friday each month.
Howards Astronomy Club
   Secretary: H. Ilett, 22 St Georges Avenue, Warblington, Havant, Hants.
   Meetings: To be notified.
Huddersfield Astronomical and Philosophical Society
   Secretary (Assistant): M. Armitage, 37 Frederick Street, Crossland Moor, Huddersfield.
   Meetings: 4A Railway Street, Huddersfield. Every Friday, 7.30 p.m.
Hull and East Riding Astronomical Society
   Secretary: A. G. Scaife, 19 Beech Road, Elloughton, East Yorks.
   Meetings: Wyke 6th Form College, Bricknell Avenue, Hull. 1st and 3rd Wednesday each month, Oct.–April, 7.30 p.m.
Ilkeston & District Astronomical Society
   Secretary: Trevor Smith, 129 Heanor Road, Smalley, Derbyshire.
   Meetings: The Friends Meeting Room, Ilkeston Museum, Ilkeston. 2nd Tuesday monthly, 7.30 p.m.
Ipswich, Orwell Astronomical Society
   Secretary: R. Gooding, 168 Ashcroft Road, Ipswich.
   Meetings: Orwell Park Observatory, Nacton, Ipswich. Wednesdays 8 p.m.
Irish Astronomical Association
   Secretary: Michael Duffy, 26 Ballymurphy Road, Belfast, Northern Ireland.
   Meetings: Room 315, Ashby Institute, Stranmills Road, Belfast. Fortnightly. Wednesdays, Sept.–April, 7.30 p.m.
Irish Astronomical Society
   Secretary: c/o PO Box 2547, Dublin 15, Eire.
Isle of Man Astronomical Society
   Secretary: James Martin, Ballaterson Farm, Peel, Isle of Man.
   Meetings: Quarterbridge Hotel, Douglas. 1st Thursday of each month, 8.30 p.m.
Isle of Wight Astronomical Society
   Secretary: J. W. Feakins, 1 Hilltop Cottages, High Street, Freshwater, Isle of Wight.
   Meetings: Unitarian Church Hall, Newport, Isle of Wight. Monthly.
Keele Astronomical Society
   Secretary: Miss Caterina Callus, University of Keele, Keele, Staffs.
   Meetings: As arranged during term time.
Kettering and District Astronomical Society
   Asst. Secretary: Steve Williams, 120 Brickhill Road, Wellingborough, Northants.
   Meetings: Quaker Meeting Hall, Northall Street, Kettering, Northants. 1st Tuesday each month. 7.45 p.m.
King's Lynn Amateur Astronomical Association
   Secretary: P. Twynman, 17 Poplar Avenue, RAF Marham, King's Lynn.
   Meetings: As arranged.
Lancaster and Morecambe Astronomical Society
   Secretary: Miss E. Haygarth, 27 Coulston Road, Bowerham, Lancaster.
   Meetings: Midland Hotel, Morecambe. 1st Wednesday each month except January. 7.30 p.m.
Lancaster University Astronomical Society
   Secretary: c/o Students Union, Alexandra Square, University of Lancaster.
   Meetings: As arranged.
Laymans Astronomical Society
   Secretary: John Evans, 10 Arkwright Walk, The Meadows, Nottingham.
   Meetings: The Popular, Bath Street, Ilkeston, Derbyshire. Monthly.
Leeds Astronomical Society
   Secretary: A. J. Higgins, 23 Montagu Place, Leeds LS8 2RQ.
   Meetings: Lecture Room, City Museum Library, The Headrow, Leeds.

Leicester Astronomical Society
Secretary: Dereck Brown, 64 Grange Drive, Glen Parva, Leicester.
Meetings: Judgemeadow Community College, Marydene Drive, Evington, Leicester. 2nd and 4th Tuesdays each month, 7.30 p.m.

Letchworth and District Astronomical Society
Secretary: Eric Hutton, 14 Folly Close, Hitchin, Herts.
Meetings: As arranged.

Limerick Astronomy Club
Secretary: Tony O'Hanlon, 26 Ballycannon Heights, Meelick, Co. Clare, Ireland.
Meetings: Limerick Senior College, Limerick, Ireland. Monthly (except June and August), 8 p.m.

Lincoln Astronomical Society
Secretary: G. Winstanley, 36 Cambridge Drive, Washingborough, Lincoln.
Meetings: The Lecture Hall, off Westcliffe Street, Lincoln. 1st Tuesday each month.

Liverpool Astronomical Society
Secretary: David Whittle, 17 Sandy Lane, Tuebrook, Liverpool.
Meetings: City Museum, Liverpool. Wednesdays and Fridays, monthly.

Loughton Astronomical Society
Meetings: Loughton Hall, Rectory Lane, Loughton, Essex. Thursdays 8 p.m.

Lowestoft and Great Yarmouth Regional Astronomers (LYRA) Society
Secretary: R. Cheek, 7 The Glades, Lowestoft, Suffolk.
Meetings: Community Wing, Kirkley High School, Kirkley Run, Lowestoft. 3rd Thursday, Sept.–May. Afterwards in School Observatory. 7.15 p.m.

Luton & District Astronomical Society
Secretary: D. Childs, 6 Greenways, Stopsley, Luton.
Meetings: Luton College of Higher Education, Park Square, Luton. Second and last Friday each month, 7.30 p.m.

Lytham St Annes Astronomical Association
Secretary: K. J. Porter, 141 Blackpool Road, Ansdell, Lytham St Annes, Lancs.
Meetings: College of Further Education, Clifton Drive South, Lytham St Annes. 2nd Wednesday monthly Oct.–June.

Macclesfield Astronomical Society
Secretary: Mrs C. Moss, 27 Westminster Road, Macclesfield, Cheshire.
Meetings: The Planetarium, Jodrell Bank, 1st Tuesday each month.

Maidenhead Astronomical Society
Secretary: c/o Chairman, Peter Hunt, Hightrees, Holyport Road, Bray, Berks.
Meetings: Library. Monthly (except July) 1st Friday.

Maidstone Astronomical Society
Secretary: Stephen James, 4 The Cherry Orchard, Haddow, Tonbridge, Kent.
Meetings: Nettlestead Village Hall, 1st Tuesday in month except July and Aug. 7.30 p.m.

Manchester Astronomical Society
Secretary: J. H. Davidson, Godlee Observatory, UMIST, Sackville Street, Manchester 1.
Meetings: At the Observatory, Thursdays, 7.30–9 p.m.

Mansfield and Sutton Astronomical Society
Secretary: G. W. Shepherd, Sherwood Observatory, Coxmoor Road, Sutton-in-Ashfield, Notts.
Meetings: Sherwood Observatory, Coxmoor Road. Last Tuesday each month, 7.45 p.m.

Mexborough and Swinton Astronomical Society
Secretary: Mark R. Benton, 61 The Lea, Swinton, Mexborough, Yorks.
Meetings: Methodist Hall, Piccadilly Road, Swinton, Near Mexborough. Thursdays, 7 p.m.

Mid-Kent Astronomical Society
Secretary: Brian A. van de Peep, 11 Berber Road, Strood, Rochester, Kent.
Meetings: Medway Teachers Centre, Vicarage Road, Strood, Rochester, Kent. Last Friday in month. Mid Kent College, Horsted. 2nd Friday in month.

Milton Keynes Astronomical Society
Secretary: The Secretary, Milton Keynes Astronomical Society, Bradwell Abbey Field Centre, Bradwell, Milton Keynes MK1 39AP.
Meetings: Alternate Tuesdays.

Moray Astronomical Society
Secretary: Richard Pearce, 1 Forsyth Street, Hopeman, Elgin, Moray, Scotland.
Meetings: Village Hall Close, Co. Elgin.

Newbury Amateur Astronomical Society
Secretary: Mrs A. Davies, 11 Sedgfield Road, Greenham, Newbury, Berks.
Meetings: United Reform Church Hall, Cromwell Road, Newbury. Last Friday of month, Aug.–May.

Newcastle-on-Tyne Astronomical Society
Secretary: C. E. Willits, 24 Acomb Avenue, Seaton Delaval, Tyne and Wear.
Meetings: Zoology Lecture Theatre, Newcastle University. Monthly.

North Aston Space & Astronomical Club
Secretary: W. R. Chadburn, 14 Oakdale Road, North Aston, Sheffield.
Meetings: To be notified.

Northamptonshire Natural History Astronomical Society
  Secretary: Dr Nick Hewitt, 4 Daimler Close, Northampton.
  Meetings: Humphrey Rooms, Castillian Terrace, Northampton. 2nd and last Monday each month.
North Devon Astronomical Society
  Secretary: P. G. Vickery, 12 Broad Park Crescent, Ilfracombe, North Devon.
  Meetings: Pilton Community College, Chaddiford Lane, Barnstaple. 1st Wednesday each month, Sept.–May.
North Dorset Astronomical Society
  Secretary: J. E. M. Coward, The Pharmacy, Stalbridge, Dorset.
  Meetings: Charterhay, Stourton, Caundle, Dorset. 2nd Wednesday each month.
North Staffordshire Astronomical Society
  Secretary: N. Oldham, 25 Linley Grove, Alsager, Stoke-on-Trent.
  Meetings: 1st Wednesday of each month at Cartwright House, Broad Street, Hanley.
North Western Association of Variable Star Observers
  Secretary: Jeremy Bullivant, 2 Beaminster Road, Heaton Mersey, Stockport, Cheshire.
  Meetings: Four annually.
Norwich Astronomical Society
  Secretary: Malcolm Jones, Tabor House, Norwich Road, Malbarton, Norwich.
  Meetings: The Observatory, Colney Lane, Colney, Norwich. Every Friday, 7.30 p.m.
Nottingham Astronomical Society
  Secretary: C. Brennan, 40 Swindon Close, Giltbrook, Nottingham.
Oldham Astronomical Society
  Secretary: P. J. Collins, 25 Park Crescent, Chadderton, Oldham.
  Meetings: Werneth Park Study Centre, Frederick Street, Oldham. Fortnightly, Friday.
Open University Astronomical Society
  Secretary: Jim Lee, c/o above, Milton Keynes.
  Meetings: Open University, Walton Hall, Milton Keynes. As arranged.
Orpington Astronomical Society
  Secretary: Miss Lucinda Jones, 263 Crescent Drive, Petts Wood, Orpington, Kent BR5 1AY.
  Meetings: Orpington Parish Church Hall, Bark Hart Road. Thursdays monthly, 7.30 p.m. Sept.–July.
Peterborough Astronomical Society
  Secretary: Sheila Thorpe, 6 Cypress Close, Longthorpe, Peterborough.
  Meetings: 1st Thursday every month at 7.30 p.m.
Plymouth Astronomical Society
  Secretary: Sheila Evans, 40 Billington Close, Eggbuckland, Plymouth.
  Meetings: Glynnis Kingdon Centre. 2nd Friday each month.
Portsmouth Astronomical Society
  Secretary: G. B. Bryant, 81 Ringwood Road, Southsea.
  Meetings: Monday. Fortnightly.
Preston & District Astronomical Society
  Secretary: P. Sloane, 77 Ribby Road, Wrea Green, Kirkham, Preston, Lancs.
  Meetings: Moor Park (Jeremiah Horrocks) Observatory, Preston. 2nd Wednesday, last Friday each month. 7.30 p.m.
The Pulsar Group
  Secretary: Barry Smith, 157 Reridge Road, Blackburn, Lancs.
  Meetings: Amateur Astronomy Centre, Clough Bank, Bacup Road, Todmorden, Lancs. 1st Thursday each month.
Reading Astronomical Society
  Secretary: Mrs Muriel Wrigley, 516 Wokingham Road, Earley, Reading.
  Meetings: St Peter's Church Hall, Church Road, Earley. Monthly (3rd Sat.), 7 p.m.
Renfrew District Astronomical Society (formerly Paisley A.S.)
  Secretary: D. Bankhead, 3c School Wynd, Paisley.
  Meetings: Coats Observatory, Oakshaw Street, Paisley. Fridays, 7.30 p.m.
Richmond & Kew Astronomical Society
  Secretary: Stewart McLaughlin, 41A Bruce Road, Mitcham, Surrey.
  Meetings: Richmond Central Reference Library, Richmond, Surrey.
Salford Astronomical Society
  Secretary: J. A. Handford, 45 Burnside Avenue, Salford 6, Lancs.
  Meetings: The Observatory, Chaseley Road, Salford.
Salisbury Astronomical Society
  Secretary: Mrs R. Collins, Mountains, 3 Fairview Road, Salisbury, Wilts.
  Meetings: Salisbury City Library, Market Place, Salisbury.
Sandbach Astronomical Society
  Secretary: Phil Benson, 8 Gawsworth Drive, Sandbach, Cheshire.
  Meetings: Sandbach School, as arranged.
Scarborough & District Astronomical Society
  Secretary: Mrs S. Anderson, Basin House Farm, Sawdon, Scarborough, N. Yorks.
  Meetings: Scarborough Public Library. Last Saturday each month, 7–9 p.m.

Scottish Astronomers Group
Secretary: G. Young c/o Mills Observatory, Balgay Park, Ancrum, Dundee.
Meetings: Bi-monthly, around the country. Syllabus given on request.

Sheffield Astronomical Society
Secretary: Mrs Lilian M. Keen, 21 Seagrave Drive, Gleadless, Sheffield.
Meetings: City Museum, Weston Park, 3rd Friday each month. 7.30 p.m.

Sidmouth and District Astronomical Society
Secretary: M. Grant, Salters Meadow, Sidmouth, Devon.
Meetings: Norman Lockyer Observatory, Salcombe Hill. 1st Monday in each month.

Solent Amateur Astronomers
Secretary: R. Smith, 16 Lincoln Close, Woodley, Romsey, Hants.
Meetings: Room 2, Oaklands Community Centre, Fairisle Road, Lordshill, Southampton. 3rd Tuesday.

Southampton Astronomical Society
Secretary: C. R. Braines, 1a Drummond Road, Hythe, Southampton.
Meetings: Room 148, Murray Building, Southampton University, 2nd Thursday each month, 7.30 p.m.

South Astronomical Society
Secretary: John C. C. Harard, Flat b, 1 Derwent Grove, East Dulwich, London.

South Downs Astronomical Society
Secretary: J. Green, 46 Central Avenue, Bognor Regis, West Sussex.
Meetings: Assembly Rooms, Chichester. 1st Friday in each month.

South-East Essex Astronomical Society
Secretary: C. Jones, 92 Long Riding, Basildon, Essex.
Meetings: Lecture Theatre, Central Library, Victoria Avenue, Southend-on-Sea. Generally 1st Thursday in month, Sept.–May.

South-East Kent Astronomical Society
Secretary: P. Andrew, 7 Farncombe Way, Whitfield, nr. Dover.
Meetings: Monthly.

South Lincolnshire Astronomical & Geophysical Society
Secretary: Ian Farley, 12 West Road, Bourne, Lincs.
Meetings: South Holland Centre, Spalding. 3rd Thursday each month, Sept.–May. 7.30 p.m.

South London Astronomical Society
Chairman: P. Bruce, 2 Constance Road, West Croydon CR0 2RS.
Meetings: Surrey Halls, Birfield Road, Stockwell, London SW4. 2nd Tuesday each month, 8 p.m.

Southport Astronomical Society
Secretary: R. Rawlinson, 188 Haig Avenue, Southport, Merseyside.
Meetings: Monthly Sept.–May, plus observing sessions.

Southport, Ormskirk and District Astronomical Society
Secretary: J. T. Harrison, 92 Cottage Lane, Ormskirk, Lancs L39 3NJ.
Meetings: Saturday evenings, monthly as arranged.

South Shields Astronomical Society
Secretary: c/o South Tyneside College, St George's Avenue, South Shields.
Meetings: Marine and Technical College. Each Thursday, 7.30 p.m.

South Somerset Astronomical Society
Secretary: G. McNelly, 11 Laxton Close, Taunton, Somerset.
Meetings: Victoria Inn, Skittle Alley, East Reach, Taunton. Last Saturday each month, 7.30 p.m.

South-West Cotswolds Astronomical Society
Secretary: C. R. Wiles, Old Castle House, The Triangle, Malmesbury, Wilts.
Meetings: 2nd Friday each month, 8 p.m. (Sept.–June).

South-West Herts Astronomical Society
Secretary: Frank Phillips, 54 Highfield Way, Rickmansworth, Herts.
Meetings: Rickmansworth. Last Friday each month, Sept.–May.

Stafford and District Astronomical Society
Secretary: Mrs L. Hodkinson, Beecholme, Francis Green Lane, Penkridge, Staffs.
Meetings: Riverside Centre, Stafford. Every 3rd Thursday, Sept.–May, 7.30 p.m.

Stirling Astronomical Society
Secretary: R. H. Lynn, 25 Pullar Avenue, Bridge of Allan, Stirling.
Meetings: Smith Museum & Art Gallery, Dumbarton Road, Stirling. 2nd Friday each month, 7.30 p.m.

Stoke-on-Trent Astronomical Society
Secretary: M. Pace, Sundale, Dunnocksfold Road, Alsager, Stoke-on-Trent.
Meetings: Cartwright House, Broad Street, Hanley. Monthly.

Sussex Astronomical Society
Secretary: Mrs C. G. Sutton, 75 Vale Road, Portslade, Sussex.
Meetings: English Language Centre, Third Avenue, Hove. Every Wednesday, 7.30–9.30 p.m. Sept.–May.

Swansea Astronomical Society
Secretary: D. F. Tovey, 43 Cecil Road, Gowerton, Swansea.
Meetings: Dillwyn Llewellyn School, John Street, Cockett, Swansea. 2nd and 4th Thursday each month at 7.30 p.m.
Tavistock Astronomical Society
Secretary: D. S. Gibbs, Lanherne, Chollacott Lane, Whitchurch, Tavistock, Devon.
Meetings: Science Laboratory, Kelly College, Tavistock. 1st Wednesday in month. 7.30 p.m.
Thames Valley Astronomical Group
Secretary: K. J. Pallet, 82a Tennyson Street, South Lambeth, London SW8 3TH.
Meetings: Irregular.
Thanet Amateur Astronomical Society
Secretary: P. F. Jordan, 85 Crescent Road, Ramsgate.
Meetings: Hilderstone House, Broadstairs, Kent. Monthly.
Torbay Astronomical Society
Secretary: R. Jones, St Helens, Hermose Road, Teignmouth, Devon.
Meetings: Town Hall, Torquay. 3rd Thursday, Oct.–May.
Tullamore Astronomical Society
Secretary: S. McKenna, 145 Arden Vale, Tullamore, Co. Offaly, Eire.
Meetings: Tullamore Vocational School, Fortnightly, Tuesdays, Oct–June. 8 p.m.
Usk Astronomical Society
Secretary: D. J. T. Thomas, 20 Maryport Street, Usk, Gwent.
Meetings: Usk Adult Education Centre, Maryport Street. Weekly, Thursdays (term dates).
Vectis Astronomical Society
Secretary: J. W. Smith, 27 Forest Road, Winford, Sandown, I.W.
Meetings: 4th Friday each month, except Dec. at Lord Louis Library Meeting Room, Newport, I.W.
Webb Society
Secretary: S. J. Hynes, 8 Cormorant Close, Sydney, Crewe, Cheshire.
Meetings: As arranged.
Wellingborough District Astronomical Society
Secretary: S. M. Williams, 120 Brickhill Road, Wellingborough, Northants.
Meetings: On 2nd Wednesday. Gloucester Hall, Church Street, Wellingborough, 7.30 p.m.
Wessex Astronomical Society
Secretary: Leslie Fry, 14 Hanhum Road, Corfe Mullen, Dorset.
Meetings: Allendale Centre, Wimborne, Dorset. 1st Tuesday of each month.
West of London Astronomical Society
Secretary: A. H. Davis, 49 Beaulieu Drive, Pinner, Middlesex HA5 1NB.
Meetings: Monthly, alternately at Hillingdon and North Harrow. 2nd Monday of the month, except August.
West Midlands Astronomical Association
Secretary: Miss S. Bundy, 93 Greenridge Road, Handsworth Wood, Birmingham.
Meetings: Dr Johnson House, Bull Street, Birmingham. As arranged.
West Yorkshire Astronomical Society
Secretary: K. Willoughby, 11 Hardisty Drive, Pontefract, Yorks.
Meetings: Rosse Observatory, Carleton Community Centre, Carleton Road, Pontefract, each Tuesday, 7.15 to 9 p.m.
Whittington Astronomical Society
Secretary: Peter Williamson, The Observatory, Top Street, Whittington, Shropshire.
Meetings: The Observatory every month.
Wolverhampton Astronomical Society
Secretary: M. Astley, Garwick, 8 Holme Mill, Fordhouses, Wolverhampton.
Meetings: Beckminster Methodist Church Hall, Birches Road, Wolverhampton. Alternate Mondays, Sept.–April.
Worcester Astronomical Society
Secretary: Arthur Wilkinson, 179 Henwick Road, St Johns, Worcester.
Meetings: Room 117, Worcester College of Higher Education, Henwick Grove, Worcester. 2nd Thursday each month.
Worthing Astronomical Society
Contact: G. Boots, 101 Ardingly Drive, Worthing, Sussex.
Meetings: Adult Education Centre, Union Place, Worthing, Sussex. 1st Wednesday each month (except August). 7.30 p.m.
Wycombe Astronomical Society
Secretary: P. A. Hodgins, 50 Copners Drive, Holmer Green, High Wycombe, Bucks.
Meetings: 3rd Wednesday each month, 7.45 p.m.
York Astronomical Society
Secretary: Simon Howard, 20 Manor Drive South, Acomb, York.
Meetings: Goddricke College, York University. 1st and 3rd Fridays.

Any society wishing to be included in this list of local societies or to update details are invited to write to the Editor (c/o Macmillan Reference, Cavaye Place, London SW10 9PG), so that the relevant information may be included in the next edition of the *Yearbook*.

STOP PRESS!

The Great Comet Collision

At the time when I write these words (24 July, 1994) we have just witnessed the spectacular end of a member of the Solar System. Comet P/Shoemaker–Levy 9 no longer exists; it has crashed to destruction upon the clouds of Jupiter.

So far as we are concerned, the story really began on 25 March 1993, when the renowned comet-hunters Eugene and Carolyn Shoemaker and David Levy were examining photographic plates taken two days earlier. They found what was described as a 'squashed comet'. It was certainly very unusual, and investigation showed it to be even stranger than it looked at first. Calculations proved that on 8 July 1992 the comet had passed within about 13,000 miles of Jupiter's cloud-tops, and had been literally torn apart, releasing sufficient dust and gas to make the shattered remnants bright enough to be seen.

At that stage the comet was already trapped in a chaotic orbit round Jupiter. When in the far part of its orbit round the Giant Planet, it was so perturbed by the pull of the Sun that its path was altered again, and it was put into a collision course. By then there were over twenty separate fragments of the original icy nucleus, spread over more than 700,000 miles (three times the distance between the Earth and the Moon), and pictures taken with the Hubble Space Telescope, showed that many of these fragments had miniature tails.

It was calculated that the first fragment would hit Jupiter on 16 July 1994, and the last on 22 July – but what would happen? Astronomers simply did not know. If the nucleus were completely fragmented, it would rain down in the manner of a shower of shrapnel and produce little effect; but a missile several miles in diameter would cause a flash and a tremendous disturbance. Sadly, all the impacts occurred on the side of Jupiter away from the Earth, but it was thought that a flash might be reflected off the Galilean satellites – and the Hubble Telescope and the Galileo space-craft might even see them 'directly'. Moreover, Jupiter spins so quickly that the impact areas would be brought into view after a few minutes.

Inevitably the astrologers and other cranks were in full cry. Astrological rubbish swamped the tabloid papers, and there was also a curious character whose name was given variously as Sofia Richmond, Sister Gabriel and Sister Marie, who believed that the impactor was Halley's Comet (!) and that it was sent as a warning to sinful mankind. Usually this sort of thing is simply amusing, but in this case it did cause some general alarm, and scientific organizations such as the BAA were forced to issue disclaimers. On one television broadcast I pointed out that the impact happened 500 million miles away, and could not possibly affect anything apart from Jupiter and the comet itself; with respect to Jupiter, I commented that it was very much like trying to stop a charging rhinoceros by throwing a baked bean at it. But as 16 July drew near, astronomers all over the world were very much on watch. It seemed possible that we would see disturbances in Jupiter's cloud deck.

This is indeed what happened, and the results were much more dramatic than anyone had dared to hope. Impacting at around 135,000 m.p.h., the largest fragments (lettered G and Q) produced explosions equivalent to about 250 million megatons of TNT. Fragment G produced a hot plume, beautifully imaged from the Hubble Telescope, and a spot as bright as the whole planet, overloading the infrared detectors on the Keck telescope at the summit of Mauna Kea in Hawaii. The plume rose to a height of over 1300 miles above the cloud-deck.

Small telescopes were quite adequate to show the results of the impact. I was fortunate in being able to use the 26-inch refractor at Herstmonceux Castle in Sussex (former home of the Royal Greenwich Observatory), which we were able to bring back into use in the nick of time. The dark patches marking the storm sites were blacker than anything I have previously seen on Jupiter, and were larger, in some cases, than the famous Red Spot. They gave every impression of being large enough and violent enough to persist for a long time – just how long, remains to be seen.

Of course there will be no permanent effect on Jupiter (remember the baked bean!) but already we have learned a great deal, both about the structure of the luckless comet and also about Jupiter's outer clouds; for example, sulphur is now known to be an important constituent. The largest fragments must have penetrated to several tens of miles, and when the results are fully analysed they may give us very important information about Jupiter's lower layers. Naturally the impact was studied at all wavelengths, and here it is worth

Sketch made on 20 July, at 20.51 GMT, using the 26-inch and 13-inch refractors at Herstmonceux Castle, magnification ×360. The storm sites appear in the south (top) part of the disk. The Great Red Spot was at this time on the far side of the planet.

noting the remarkable results obtained by the pupils at Taunton School in Somerset, who have set up their own elaborate radio astronomy observatory.

Of course the results are only just starting to come in, and this account is preliminary only; there will be a full report in the 1996 *Yearbook*. Meanwhile, we have been privileged to witness an event which has never been observed before. Comet Shoemaker–Levy 9 is dead, but it still has a great deal to tell us.